Plan for Happy

A step-by-step guide to growing your money

Adam Walkom

Clink Street

Published by Clink Street Publishing 2023

Copyright © 2023

First edition.

The author asserts the moral right under the Copyright, Designs and Patents Act 1988 to be identified as the author of this work.

ISBN:
978-1-915229-39-7 - paperback
978-1-915229-40-3 - ebook

For Chloe & all my family

CONTENTS

HOW TO THINK ABOUT YOUR FINANCES

PLANNING

SAVING

INVESTING

GOING FURTHER

SUPPLEMENTARY SECTION

CHAPTER 1

It all Starts with a Thought

"Oh shit, not again!" was my first thought.

"What happened?" I asked my father who was clearly upset and disconsolate having to break the news to his 21-year-old son.

"I got a margin call mate," he started, trying to hold back tears, my mother looking on rather helplessly with all the emotion in her eyes "I had to sell everything and then some. Everything that I built back from selling the shop is gone."

At this point as a 21-year-old I had no idea what a margin call was. Most people today, to their fortune, don't know what one is, but I could tell then it wasn't good. My family had been through the ups and downs financially and it had all seemed like it was getting better. My father was working for a large investment bank in Australia and was seemingly paid very well. Then 2008 and the global financial crises hit and global share markets started falling… hard. My father had received shares in his employer and was so confident about the prospects of further growth, he had used these shares and others he owned as collateral to borrow money, to buy more shares. This is called a margin loan and you can see where this is going. When markets fell aggressively, the issuer of the loan has the right to call it in – a margin call – which means you need to find the money to pay back the loan, no matter what the shares are. Normally this means selling at the worst possible time and this was no exception for my father.

"What are you going to do?" I asked.

"I don't know," responded my father in exasperation and it was at that very moment I realised the truism that every child understands to their shock at some point in their life about their parents.

I saw he was human.

I'm a financial planner and I have a very simple reason for writing this book. I do not want anyone to go through what I, my parents and the rest of the family had to go through.

I want everyone reading this book to understand the link between your overall financial situation and your overall mental health and happiness. I want to you to *Plan For Happy*. It's not rocket science, it just takes a bit of thought. But, that's what I'm here to help you with.

Personal finance is perhaps the most important topic anyone could ever learn about for their and their family's personal wellbeing… yet nobody teaches it to you. There are no classes in school or university. I remember in my Year 11 accounting class in Australia being taught how to write a cheque. Three stars to my school for effort, but that was really no foundation for life in the big and potentially hostile world that surrounds personal finance today.

We all face considerable pressure in our day-to-day lives and financial pressure is one of the biggest issues we all face. There are many studies around which show the links between financial stress and depression. The charity Mind highlight common mental health symptoms associated with money problems such as anxiety and panic, sleep problems and feeling lonely and isolated[1]. Managing your finances properly has never been more important.

One way to think about this is to consider financial planning the anathema to the pressures of modern-day marketing. "Buy now pay later", "live for today" or "use our reward scheme" are all different versions of credit marketing that try to get you to spend money that you don't have, which will cost you significantly more in the future. Financial planning is the complete opposite – it's about saving money you don't have, which means

---

1   https://www.mind.org.uk/information-support/tips-for-everyday-living/money-and-mental-health/the-link-between-money-and-mental-health/#money-can-affect-mental-health

you can spend significantly more in the future. Yet bizarrely, financial planners seem to have a worse reputation – perhaps the industry needs a greater marketing budget?

Put simply, everyone, that is every single person in this world needs financial help. They just haven't worked out they need it yet. Budgeting, planning, investing, understanding markets are all vital skills for your financial well-being, yet who really understands how to do it? Friends, parents, YouTube? More importantly who shows you how to do it? The difference between what most people do with their money and what they can do to maximise their money is huge. And I want to show you how you can make that leap.

I work with around 150 clients and help them plan their financial future. Sounds easy, but it isn't. Not only is everybody's personal financial situation different, but so are their goals and needs. Just to complicate things, the rules and regulations around tax and investments change every year. So how does anybody who doesn't talk to an expert have a chance?

You want to know the best thing about this job? Helping people understand what is possible. So many people have their head down and it's all work, family, work, friends, work as it has been since school. Most of my clients I would call "high achievers" because that is just the way they're wired. The way I work with my clients is about getting them to really stop and understand what is going on. And most people find this a revelatory process. So, when I get a potential client in a room and start mapping out their financial future on the screen, showing where they are today and most likely where they are headed, in tends to spark some interest. I then continue and normally say "If you do these three things today, I can confidently get you here in ten years' time", and at this point the physical changes in the client start to happen. Their eyes widen, the shoulders drop and the mouth opens. "Really?" is the normal response. "We can spend that much?" or "I can retire then?" And at that point I can tell they get it. In their own mind they have reached their "Happy Place" as I call it. The place where they feel they can relax about their finances. I love that moment. Having a greater understanding of your finances has significant benefits – financially and more important mentally. All because we have planned for Happy.

In contrast to the mental health issues raised above with money pressures, the opposite is also true. A recent 2021 study titled "Experienced well-being rises with income, even above $75,000 per year" from researchers at Wharton School for Business at the University of Pennsylvania suggested that higher incomes are associated with both feeling better day-to-day and being more satisfied with life overall.[2] Previous studies had concluded that happiness tended to plateau above this $75,000 income level,[3] which this study refutes. The study concludes there was no evidence of any particular income threshold at which happiness stopped going up. Equally important, in my view, is having an understanding of the bigger picture and direction of our financial lives. There is no point striving for more and more money just for the sake of it. You need to understand what you can do with it.

Planning your finances is taking a top-down view on everything. It's flying above your situation and work/family and daily busyness to give you a bigger vision – a strategic plan. Most importantly, it changes people's lives.

How many decisions do you make in your life that have a fundamental impact on your future? Speaking to a financial planner is one of them.

The best way to find a financial planner is to ask your friends or colleagues who they use. Personal recommendations from someone you trust are the best because, like going to a doctor or hairdresser, your relationship with your financial planner is very personal and chemistry needs to exist between you. The other way to find a suitable planner is internet research, but make sure you research specific characteristics about you. For example, my firm helps lawyers, management consultants and investment bankers. We focus specifically on these people because we have

---

2   https://www.pnas.org/doi/10.1073/pnas.2016976118
3   http://content.time.com/time/magazine/article/0,9171,2019628,00.html

specific knowledge about their industries that adds extra value to them. Many other firms focus on many other specific areas – sportspeople, doctors, dentists are some examples. Have a search on the internet and see.

The key factor though which many people come back to is cost and yes, financial planners have to charge, that is how we run a business. The costs can be less than you think and I would encourage you to seriously consider this as an investment in your future, but it is not for everyone. I understand that many people simply can't afford what we need to charge to cover the costs of a) running our business and b) what the regulator keeps forcing us to do compliance-wise (but that is a whole other story). The financial planning industry also has had a challenging reputation over the years as pushy product sellers. Historically this is deserved, but the industry has been significantly cleaned up over the last ten years and you now need specific qualifications to get in, and importantly stay in, the industry.

If you don't want to commit the time or money to speaking to a financial planner, then this book is the next best thing.

This book is a how-to guide to get your finances sorted out, build your understanding of markets and investments and provide you with more money in the longer term than you would have had otherwise. Lofty goals, I know, but well worth the price you paid for the book!

When you finish reading this book, you will have a complete understanding of the following

- How your upbringing and background has determined the way you think about money, and what you can do about it
- How to plan your spending in a way that controls your budget but allows you to buy all the important things you want
- How to increase your monthly surplus income while doing more of the things you enjoy doing

- How to plan your investments to match your short, medium and long-term goals
- How to let the stock market do the heavy lifting for you and build wealth over the long-term that far exceeds your expectations
- And, finally, how to have complete confidence in yourself and your plan and feel the burden of your and your family's financial future lift from your shoulders

Does that sound good to you? If so, then let's dive in.

When most people thing about financial planning, or their finances in general, they just think about the basics – savings, investments, pensions etc. These are all necessary tools for success in achieving your Plan for Happy but they are just that – they are tools that we use. The best way to describe this is like thinking about an iceberg.

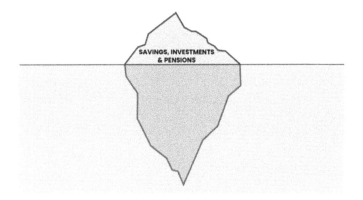

We know that with any iceberg, what we can see on top is around less than one-fifth of the true size and majesty of what lies beneath the waterline. When I think about helping someone create their Plan for Happy, I consider savings, investments, pensions etc all the "above the line" items. They are simply tools that we use. But to really build a great financial plan, we instead need to think of the outcomes that this plan will give them. A pension itself won't give anybody an outcome, but how about giving someone full visibility of their current and projected financial situation so they can really understand where they are today financially and what the future looks like if they stay on this path? I think that sounds a lot better.

Then how about if we can give you an optimised investment strategy, based on your exact plans and needs of not only how much money you're going to need or want when you retire, but exactly when those funds will be required at any point in your life for things like house renovations or school fees? And remember, retirement is not how it used to be so the strategy will reflect your personal retirement decisions around easing back from work slowly or not at all.

Finally, what about if we could show you a way through saving and investment that could maximise your wealth, no matter what level you are starting at? No matter if you're starting with £1,000 or £1 million, by taking active, regular steps and investing in the correct way for you, we can ensure that you achieve the maximum possible over the long-term.

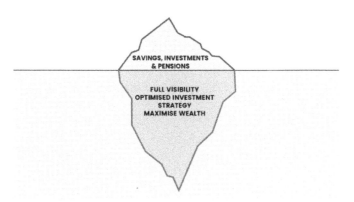

Does that sound better than putting together a plan just showing saving, investments and pensions? I think it does.

But again, these are just outcomes. What do they mean for you? What does it mean to have a complete understanding of your finances, an optimised investment strategy or to maximise wealth?

This is where we need to go deeper. To really get down to the depths and see the true underlying beauty of the iceberg. To really understand your "Why?" in terms of not just your finances, but your overall life and goals and plans. What makes you tick? What drives you? But most importantly, what makes you happy? We think your financial situation makes up a big part of this.

Which is why it is so important to *Plan For Happy*.

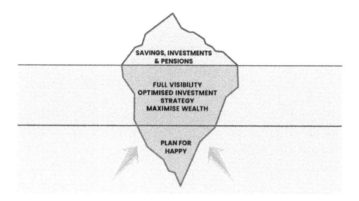

The point of this exercise is to demonstrate that in order to achieve a sense of personal fulfilment with your finances, to really feel at peace, we need to go a lot deeper than just thinking of savings, investments and pensions. We need to really drill down into your background, motives and fears to help you *Plan For Happy* and find your Happy Place.

Let me start with a story. There was a young man (let's say aged 25) who worked at an investment bank. He was paid very well for what he did and loved living in London. He went out, enjoyed himself, met lots of new and interesting people and had a great time. Did he spend frivolously? Not always, but on many occasions yes. Could he have spared £100 per week to put away into savings? Yes. But did he? Absolutely not. Perhaps you won't be surprised to hear that young man was me.

Unlike the rest of us, for a young investment bank graduate £100 per week may not seem much, but this is where maths and the joy of compounding comes in. Even if I had put away £100 a week for ten years and then let the balance just grow until I was 60. Any guess what it would be worth then?

Just over £134,000.

Do you think I'm kicking myself for that? Of course I am, but I just didn't know. I wasn't aware of the impact as nobody had shown me and I didn't have a plan or a strategy around it. I don't want you to make the same mistakes I made.

I don't need to tell you that life is ridiculously busy. Work, family, social. How many of us end each day thinking "Wow, I was really bored today?" Not many I think. At the same time, our poor primitive brains are bombarded with the cleverest, most complex advertising messages designed to either hijack our emotions or get us to spend money, or worse – both. Social media, television, newspapers, magazines all exist just for one reason and one reason only – to get your attention so somebody can sell you something.

So how do we possibly cope with all this – a busy mind that is being constantly attacked by external forces?

Well, it's hard enough at the best of times, but simply having a plan and a direction of where you want to go financially gives you a big head start. Having an overarching goal, such as 'I want to retire with £1 million in the bank' or 'I want to buy a new house in five years', and really having that ingrained into your brain can be a powerful shield against the modern world.

This is for two reasons. The first is that it allows you to put structures in place that take away some of the surplus income that you may otherwise spend – call this forced saving. Think of my extra £100 that should have otherwise gone into my pension. The second, more important reason, is that it gives your brain a chance to fight back and say "No, I don't want to make that random purchase, because I have something bigger and more important that I'm working towards."

That is why you make a plan.

But before we dive further into creating the plan, let's take a step back and see what is the biggest influence on our personal financial philosophy – our upbringing.

CHAPTER 2

The Emotional Context of Money

In this chapter you will learn

- *What money means to me and my history*
- *How money actually does influence happiness, but not in the way you may think*
- *Understand more about your own background and how it influences your current approach to money*

What money means to me – my story

What does money mean to you? Does it mean safety? Security? Living? Everyone has a slightly different answer. If you have enough money, you can buy whatever you need. If you don't, there are some things you might very much want that you're going to have to go without. But money is much more than that. There are very few people for whom it does not have a significant emotional context. (When I say, "very few people," what I actually mean is: I've never met one. I don't suppose you have, either.) And that emotional context comes from our past. For most of us, it's probably rooted in our childhood. Mine certainly is.

I grew up in Melbourne, Australia. My father had an excellent and well-paid job and I and my two brothers were educated at a private school where break-time conversation might be around the new boat one of the pupil's fathers was considering buying. A nice life, you might think, and it was. Very middle-class. Very prosperous.

And then, in 1991, my father was made redundant. Up to this point, my mother had only worked part time. That had to change, and she and my father set up a bookshop. They did this under the guidance of a friend who was already in the business; nevertheless, it did not go terribly well. Money changed from being something to which no one ever gave a thought to something that was always the source of worry. Our parents probably thought they succeeded in keeping the worry from us, but they didn't. We were well aware of it, especially when the house had to be sold to fund the business and we moved into rented accommodation.

As young people growing up the issue of money and wealth becomes more and more prevalent the older we become. We simply cannot help it as society is wired this way. We see it in the media, we notice it in our friends and gradually relate it back to ourselves and our families. If you are a parent, I would encourage you to discuss money with your children. As our awareness of money and wealth increases, yet like so many things during our childhood, our understanding may not. A study by the Children and Youth Services review in 2018 concluded that "financial literacy (in young people) was associated mainly with understanding the value of savings and discussing money matters with parents."[4]

Back to my story, it appeared to get better for my parents, and therefore for us, when my father was offered his old job back. He accepted and my mother took over the whole running of the shop which limped on for another year before they sold it, losing pretty well everything they had from the house sale as well as the redundancy payment. Well, these things happen and they moved on.

And then, in 2008, stock markets crashed around the world and the story in the previous chapter took place. Now it was all gone. We had gone from abundance to being extremely hard-up,

4   Dolores Moreno-Herrero, Manuel Salas-Velasco, José Sánchez-Campillo, Factors that influence the level of financial literacy among young people: The role of parental engagement and students' experiences with money matters, Children and Youth Services Review, Volume 95, 2018, Pages 334–351, https://doi.org/10.1016/j.childyouth.2018.10.042.

back to something amounting to sufficiency if not abundance, and then to being hard up once more.

I'm certainly not looking for sympathy here as over my career I have heard hundreds of similar stories. Money and wealth (and life for that matter) is rarely linear – nothing happens in a straight line. You may have a similar story where either you, or your parents, have been made redundant, or businesses failing or relationships ending that causes not just families but assets to be split up. All these situations leave their mark on us emotionally and this comes through in terms of how we view and spend our money. This is certainly nothing to be ashamed about and in fact, I believe it goes a long way to give you a healthy respect for money.

So that's my background and given my career is understanding people's financial background I know situations like this are very common.

This background has left me with the significant impression that if my parents had more financial help, heaven forbid spoke to a financial planner, they would not have made the same decisions they did. My single most prominent objective is making sure that my wife and children will always be looked after, come what may. I have also extended that into becoming a financial planner because I want to make sure other people also have every opportunity to make the right decisions by receiving the right advice.

Perhaps I am an extreme example but my reasons for raising this are two-fold. First, I want you to think about your upbringing and how your background has influenced your attitudes to money. We will do a little exercise on this shortly. Secondly, if you are a parent, I want you to consider the influence your situation and attitudes are having on your children and how you can potentially help that. My experience with my own parent's financial ups and downs taught me that children, once they reach their teens, may never do what you tell them, but they will learn from what they see you doing. As a father, I need constantly to remind myself of this fact. Setting an example of how to look after money properly is a very good idea – for yourself and your children.

What does money mean to you?

This book isn't about me. It's about you. It's about your story, your background, but most importantly, your future. To put together a financial plan that is potentially both realistic and successful we need to help you clarify the emotional context your relationship with money started.

This may sound serious but it's not that bad. It's simply trying to get you to be aware and notice those influences. A good therapist will ask us to analyse our current habits and, without beating ourselves up, will ask us to notice and say, "That's interesting, I wonder why I do that?" Maybe you grew up in a household where your parents had very different ideas about money which caused tension. Maybe you grew up in a well-off household, but had far wealthier neighbours/friends which your parents were always trying to compare themselves too. It is a commonly known psychological trait that our attitudes end up trying to right the perceived wrongs of our own upbringing. I know mine does. Everybody has a story and everybody's story influences their habits and attitudes today.

In a Forbes article, Prudy Gourguechon highlights the most important emotions when it comes to money – fear, guilt, shame and envy.[5] Of those mentioned, the emotion I find most interesting is shame, because shame causes us to shy away from something or avoid it. Think about it, if you're ashamed of something, you are simply going to not do it. A few common examples she highlights are:

- I don't have enough money.
- I've avoided thinking about my finances.
- I've avoided doing what I'm supposed to do about finances (creating a safety net, planning for retirement, sensible budgeting).

---

5   https://www.forbes.com/sites/prudygourguechon/2019/02/25/the-psychology-of-money-what-you-need-to-know-to-have-a-relatively-fearless-financial-life/

- I'm really ignorant about all of this.
- I spend too much.
- I buy stuff when I'm unhappy.

You may recognise some of these emotions in your own life. Each of these are excuses we tell ourselves and potentially almost label ourselves saying "That's just me." My point is it may be you now but a) that has come from somewhere in your past and b) it doesn't have to be you in the future.

To help I have created a very simple test that hopefully will help you understand your own emotional background to money a little more.

How feelings affect spending patterns

When we feel well-off, we tend to feel more confident but that can also lead to overspending depending on our background. Try this. Answer the following questions by scoring them from 1 – 5, with 1 being the lowest and 5 the highest:

1. Growing up, how well-off did you feel your family was? (Score 1 for not at all and 5 for extremely)
2. Also at that time, how well-off did you feel your family was compared with your schoolmates, neighbours, cousins and others around you? (Score 1 for not at all and 5 for extremely)
3. Were you ever aware of tension between your parents over money? (Score 1 for very aware and 5 for not at all aware)
4. How do you handle your credit cards? (Score 1 for repay in full every month and 5 for permanently run a balance close to my limit)
5. Now apply Question 4 to your bank account (Score 1 for always in credit and 5 for permanently overdrawn at close to the limit)

6. Would you describe yourself as an untidy or disorganised person? By which I mean both at work and in your personal life? Do you keep an untidy workplace? Kitchen? Bedroom? (Score 1 for not at all untidy and 5 for shambolic)

If you scored mostly 1s and 2s, with perhaps a single 3, you've never felt overly well-off but you understand the importance of money. Your spending decisions tend to be frugal and you have conservative expectations. This book will benefit you because the key to creating a successful financial plan is discipline – and you've got that.

If you scored mostly 2s and 3s with perhaps a single 4, you have a relatively middle-class upbringing with some money around. This has the potential sometimes to be dangerous because your spending expectations may exceed your current income, but you've got enough experience to set this right. This book will help you because it will keep you on track and perhaps stop your spending running out of control.

If you scored mostly 4s and 5s, there have been periods in your life when you've had the perception of being well-off. You also have tended to spend those funds, so for you saving and investing may be a problem – you can't invest what you don't have. The first step is the most important and you made it when you picked up this book. The benefit will come in the future plans we make together through the rest of the book.

Bring your partner along with you on the journey

If you're in a relationship, then at this point I'm going to ask you to stop reading. The reason is that every relationship, even if we don't consider it does from the outside, has some sort of financial component to it. I found this out when my wife and I were looking to move back to Australia from London. I'm Australian, so there was no issue for me, but she is a Brit so we had to get her a partner visa. But we're married I thought, so it should just be a forgone conclusion. Wrong. When deciding whether to authorise a partner visa the Australian immigration office's primary focus is one single type of evidence – not a marriage certificate, not photos, not declarations of love – they just look for financial history. They want to see evidence of money going backwards and forwards between the couple as that type of history cannot be falsified – all the others can.

For a relationship to be long-lasting, healthy and open, then our true attitudes to money and finances need to be open and discussed. How common is it to hear couples have an argument about money? A little too common if you ask me.

If you want to begin this journey, then you need to have your partner alongside you. My suggestion is that you ask your partner to also complete the above exercise on spending. Just please don't expect your partner to have the same answers as you – remember we all have different upbringings and perspectives we're bringing to this. Use it as a chance to start a discussion and work through this book together. Remember you're looking to *Plan For Happy*. This will be very hard to achieve if you're in a relationship and having arguments about money.

It is also important to make the point that just having more money doesn't solve all your problems. When asked about how his life had changed after Nirvana became successful the late Kurt Cobain said "The money is just one less thing to worry about. You can't buy happiness." And unfortunately for Kurt, and for the rest of us who loved his music, we know how that ended up. For me the key point is not the actual money, but the control of it. The understanding that money can have a purpose and be an enormously powerful factor in improving lives. We just need to look after and control it before it controls us.

Now that you have more understanding of what made you the person you are today, at any rate financially, we can look to the future and help you change that person life has shaped to this point.

This next stage is really fun. When I work with my clients, I get inspiration from this quote.

Antoine de Saint-Exupéry said:

"If you want to build a ship, don't drum up the men to gather wood, divide the work, and give orders. Instead, teach them to yearn for the vast and endless sea."

We stop smoking because we want to be healthy. We buy a bike because we want to be fit. And we get our spending under control because our dream is of a secure future.

CHAPTER 3

Focus on Happiness

In this chapter you will learn

- *The importance of planning not solely on your finances, but focusing instead on happiness.*
- *How the journey is more important than the destination.*
- *The 2 key drivers of happiness that I have learned through experience with clients over many years.*

The early parts of this book focus on helping you think about and articulate your Happy Place. This is the sort of retirement nirvana where we want to put ourselves in the future, by making active decisions around our finances today. Many people, and particularly high achievers, who are able to define this clearly in their minds, have a clearer framework which they work towards and encourages them to make the right decisions because they have that long-term goal in mind.

But let us remember the title of this book, Plan For Happy. We're not necessarily planning to have the most money in the world, we're not even planning to be "rich" (however you want to define that). We're planning to be happy. And you want me to tell you the secret to this, that I've discovered through years of working with clients to help achieve this goal? Everyone's level of happiness is relative and can change over time.

Simply by understanding that happiness - which in this context we can also reframe as contentment with your financial situation - is a relative state and can be changed over time, giving you an enormous advantage over the majority of people out their slaving away and simply hoping for some sort of successful retirement.

The idea that happiness is just in our minds is a rather Stoic attitude that Ryan Holiday brings to life best in his great book Discipline is Destiny.[6] Using just money, or an amount of assets, to define your happiness is dangerous. Ryan says:

"No amount of money is ever going to truly free you. But being less dependent, caring less about money? That will free you right now."

I love that idea.

That also helps us focus more on the day-to-day part of life. The important part of what actually is in front of us right now. You ask anyone who has just been diagnosed with a significant illness and they will tell you the days before that they had "nothing" to worry about. They long for those days to return. Yet, those "nothing" days for the majority of us are now – right here, today – and yet we still worry, stress, think "in the future, when I've made it, I'll be happy".

Naval Ravikant has expressed similar thoughts.

"We all are chasing Wealth, Happiness and Health. We just do it in the wrong order."[7]

Naval has an interesting idea which even includes health being the priority and thinking about that, it makes sense. Without your health, it is much harder to be happier and content with your life. The key point we all know about looking after your health is that it is one area that certainly cannot be postponed into the future. Living healthily starts today and has very similar compounding affects to your finances. Continuous bad decisions, or no decisions around your health – like smoking, drinking too much, eating junk - and that ends up being a very slippery slope you fall down. The flipside is also true and

6   Holiday, Ryan. *Discipline is Destiny.* Profile Books. 2022
7   Jorgensen, Eric. *The Almanac of Naval Ravikant.*

the same goes for when we think about wealth. We will see in a future chapter that this act of making positive decisions today around your finances can put you on the path towards your Happy Place.

When I talk to my clients, we often discuss their financial journey or the path that they're on. What I try to emphasise with them is that the journey is not about the destination. It's not just about waking up one day to find you have £1 million in the bank and thinking "Ah, I've made it". It's about crafting the life you want to live before this, using all the resources you have and making them work for you instead of the other way around.

Ryan Holiday, again, in his book deals with this.

"The problem is that many of us tell ourselves that someday we will be beyond this, that if we can just earn enough, we won't have to consider any of it…. Because we'll be "good", we'll have "arrived". Here's the thing. This never happens."

There is nothing wrong with thinking about the long-term and planning to be financially content at that time. That's what this book is all about. My point really is that that should not be pined for at all costs. We shouldn't wish away our current life for some sunset-filled vision of the future where we think we'll have "made it".

Because the other thing to remember is that "it" changes. What we plan for at age 40 and what we actually want when we get to 65 can be two very different scenarios. Life changes, priorities change, there is illness, success, grief and everything in between that we all contend with and we cannot deny that this will have at least some sort of significant impact on what drives our future determinant of happiness. This is not an excuse though. It certainly doesn't mean we shouldn't plan for our future. Again, it's just understanding the nature and context of making plans for 20,30 and 40+ years time. These plans will rarely come to fruition EXACTLY as we imagine them. But that is just life and that shouldn't stop us imagining, because it's the act of imagining and imprinting that Happy Place in our mind that drives the active and positive decision-making today.

How does this help you? It helps because potentially that big figure, dream scenario you initially imagined may not actually be what really would make you happy. There are many people who would say spending their hours sitting by a pool doing nothing is their dream retirement. Is it really though? Whilst great to start with, I know I would get bored stiff after about 3 days. And when I get bored, I annoy my wife, and then nobody is happy.

I'm not sure when it happened but the generally accepted Anglo-Saxon idea of "retirement" is playing golf regularly and taking long walks. Why? Perhaps, like most things in the Anglo-Saxon world, it stems from the British Victorian times where working life was hard labour and upon retirement that just stopped. In that time what normally followed was a swift death. But those times are over. My guess is that most of you spend more time on a keyboard than anywhere else for almost every day of your life. Think about that for a second. This is where a significant number of people spend the majority of their peak years. There are many mental challenges of working in the 21st century, but hard labour has diminished significantly. So why is there still the stereotype of a "perfect" retirement is one where we totally stop and our mind and bodies turn to mush?

So, bringing this back to you again. Why not consider some part-time work later into life in thinking about your Happy Place? Why not plan to work until 70, 75 even 80 on a part-time role, doing something you love, helping people, being involved in the community? This may be voluntary, which is fantastic, or it may involve getting paid. With the state pension paying around £10,000 per year in 2023 and doing basic work earning around £10,000 per year, you are starting your retirement with an income of £20,000 before you even need to draw anything else. That amount could cover food and bills. Even better if you're married, then you both will receive the state pension, adding another £10,000 to bring the total to £30,000 for a couple. I know many couples who are perfectly happy living off that amount. You may not think that will be you, but at least you know it is possible. This brings us to an important point, our individual view on what it costs us to be happy and what drives this.

We talked in Chapter 2 about the emotional context of money. How our upbringing influences our attitude towards money and finance. The same rule applies to planning for happy. Our view on happiness is also driven as much by our upbringing as our view on money. Think of this as an example. What is the difference between a Rolex watch and a Swatch. Both fulfil their main functional purpose almost identically. They are both very good at telling the time. For some people, that is where it stops. "Why would I ever buy a Rolex?" some ask themselves, "a normal watch tells the same time." However, for others, a Rolex is so much more. It is a status symbol, a message to the outside world, a sign that you've made "it". Your upbringing will have a significant impact on which side of the coin you believe. The exercise you did around your spending habits offers a clue as to how you would think about this. Please remember, there is no right answer. There is nothing wrong with wanting a Rolex, they are beautiful watches and can be considered jewellery. Humans have been wearing jewellery since the ancient Egyptians which indicates there is potentially some biological or evolutionary need to wear shiny, precious things. There is nothing wrong with wanting to show off a status symbol of your wealth and this, for you, may drive significant happiness. For others, it may not, and that is ok as well. The status symbol part of this discussion brings in the next point I want to make – happiness is relative.

There was a famous meme that went across social media around 2 or 3 years ago. It showed footage of a beautiful boat moored in some tropical paradise. Suddenly, a much larger boat looms past and the attention of the camera is moved away to that boat. The camera lingers on the larger boat for another few seconds, before an even larger boat, more than twice the size of the second boat, comes in to view and goes past it. The caption of the video uses the somewhat pithy line of "how an investment banker feels about his bonus" implying the initial joy an investment banker may feel about his/her bonus is soon dwarfed by the realisation there is always someone who is earning more than him/her. The meme may be focused on a very small number of individuals – being investment bankers and their bonuses. But it can be applied at every different level. We constantly compare ourselves to our peers, even if we try and not do it.

This doesn't just relate to finance. The Psychology Today website published an article by Dr John G. Cottone entitled "Happiness: Is it all relative?"[8]. In the article Dr Cotonne describes two different clients of his – Omar and Lena – who come from very different backgrounds and, you guessed it, have very different happiness levels with their situations. His conclusion is that we don't tend to think about or compare our situation versus THE world, that is simply too abstract and too big for us to take in. What we do is compare to OUR world. Our world is the small number of connections that we have. The closer the connection, the higher the influence upon us.

Let us bring this back to you again. Think about your closest contacts. How do you feel you try to match up with them? Even if you have never thought about it before are you trying to keep up with the Joneses? Does that impact your decision-making and even potentially your overall happiness?

Nasim Nicholas Taleb sums up the concept of relative wealth with this rather blunt quote.

To feel rich, socialise with poor people. To feel poor, socialise with rich people[9].

We've talked a lot in this chapter about how being happy is a relative state and is not just related to your financial situation. We've also discussed that our own version or goal of happiness can change over time, based on our own internal shifts in thinking but also external influences around us. Whilst sounding more complicated this is good news. It means it's not just the numbers in the bank or investments, but it is actually what is going on in our own minds. And in our minds is where we begin the next chapter – to dream of that Happy Place.

---

8   https://www.psychologytoday.com/us/blog/the-cube/202201/happiness-is-it-all-relative [accessed 26th February 2023]

9   Taleb, Nassim Nicholas. *The Bed of Procrustes.*

CHAPTER 4

Looking Forwards

In this chapter you will learn

- *To imprint your ideal Happy Place in your mind*
- *To understand the four future scenarios you face*
- *The importance of taking active decisions and not letting things drift.*

Now you know who you are. Who do you want to be?

The exercise we've been through in Chapter 2 was to establish what our financial habits have been up to now, and where they have left us. Think of that as the backward-looking part of this book. Now let's look forward. Imagine yourself 15, 20, 25, 30 years from now.

One of the most powerful ways we can change is to set clear goals and then put a plan in place to get there. I know most people cringe when they hear the word "goal-setting" so let us reframe it this way. Let's not set goals at this point, let's simply dream of your Happy Place.

Imagine it's 20 years from now, imagine you've achieved the things you dreamed about – so where are you? Who are you with? What did you do this morning? What are you doing for lunch? What have you planned for the afternoon and evening? Let your imagination go wild. Most importantly as you dream remember this: You are happy. You have achieved what you wanted to achieve financially, professionally whatever. This is your dream – you don't need any excuses. Just think about it. More importantly, write it down. It's important – probably the single most important thing in our lives, because we won't get anywhere if we don't know where we're going.

You can download our easy to use PDF from the website here (www.adamwalkom.com)

This is my Happy Place. What is life like?
Where are you? What country? What can you see?
Who are you with?
What did you do today? How about this evening?

Do you want to be living in a seafront apartment in Spain? Living in a motorhome on a New Zealand beach? Running a successful business? Owning a grand house in the Cotswolds with children running around? Don't think about the money at this point because we will come back to that. This exercise is simply focused on your ideal scenario – or Happy Place.

Everyone will have a different idea of how they want to be living at some future time. The purpose of this book is to make it possible for *you* to achieve whatever *your* aim is.

If you cannot say exactly what you want to be doing, don't worry. This is normal. There are many times when I have this conversation with prospective clients and they just shift in their seat and look slightly embarrassed as they say "I don't know, I've never really thought about it."

Just make a guess as it can always, and probably will, change over the years. Just think about how your own attitudes have changed in the last five or ten years. Retiring to a villa in Ibiza may sound idyllic to you as a later-life choice to you whilst you are in your 20s, however by the time you reached 50 that may have changed.

I'm just asking you to have a go. Stop for a minute, close your eyes, and think about your Happy Place.

The 4 future states of you

So let's begin a little exercise now. You've established your dream scenario. Hopefully you've got a really clear vision of this in your mind's eye. We're going to use this scenario as an input in a little model to think about the future.

See the diagram below. It shows where we are today and the only thing we can know for sure – that as the passage of time passes you will arrive in some future state. For your sake I hope that is the Happy Place we've established previously.

However, let us imagine a few other scenarios now. This is real life, right? Let us imagine another future scenario where things have worked out well, but just not quite up to the Happy Place we've imagined. Life is ok here, but not quite as good as it could have been.

Now let's imagine another scenario where life has just about worked out Just OK. Again, Just OK is slightly worse than the previous Good, but still a fair way off the original ideal scenario at the top.

Then finally, again let's be realistic here, for some unfortunate people, life will hand them a bad deal. Incidents will occur and not go their way and they will end up in what we call Crisis.

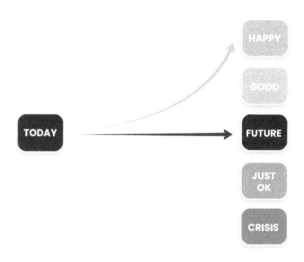

Crisis is about as bad as it gets. My editor didn't want me to be negative, however I pushed back to say this is such an important aspect of financial planning. We need to understand how bad things can get in order to make sure we plan to avoid it. The thing with ending up in Crisis is that you don't just wake one day and find yourself there. Your path from today to Crisis is a downward curve that gets worse and accelerates as time goes on because of compounding. Like in maths, compounding may not seem like much at the start, but very quickly can spiral out of control.

We call this Drift. Drift is letting things slide. Drift is not planning. Drift is letting events control you instead of you controlling events. Think about the credit card debt cycle that you or someone you know may have got themselves into. Once you start down that path, it's very hard to break. By letting things drift your time moves from Today potentially down to Crisis.

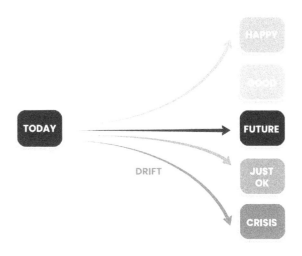

Drift not only occurs heading to the Crisis scenario, but also to the Just OK scenario, it is not quite as pronounced. Again, this is where potentially some things have gone better, but it's still not a great place to be.

The good news however, is the compounding affect that causes Drift, works in reverse as well. By making Decisions. Decisiveness gets you on the right path to success. Decisiveness means following the plan we're going to create in this book. Decisiveness means keeping your spending below your earnings. Taking the right active decisions at the right time is how you start heading towards your Good scenario. And those active decisions can have a positive impact on the next decision and so on, hence the compounding turning around in this scenario and beginning to work in your favour.

Then finally we have our Happy Place again – remember that? This is where I start to let you in on the secret of how to achieve it. The way to achieve that Happy Place is making active decisions in terms of your life and finances. That's it. It's about taking control and not letting it or you sit idly by. The good news is that it doesn't necessarily cost any money to make these active decisions, it just requires ambition and – you guessed it – planning.

The difference between achieving your Happy Place or things sliding into Crisis is the difference between Decisions and Drift.

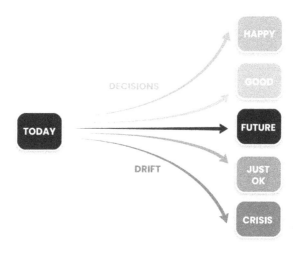

Let's consider your own situation at the moment. Where do you think you sit? Are you taking all the active decisions possible to achieve your Happy scenario. Or are you letting things Drift? Let's consider you're on the Good or Just OK path at the moment. Given the compounding effect, how long do you think it would take you to notice that you are starting to slide off that path in a downward direction by letting things drift? One year? Three years? Five years? The good news is that normally you can rectify what course you are on, you can jump lines. But, the longer you take, the gaps between then scenarios get bigger and bigger.

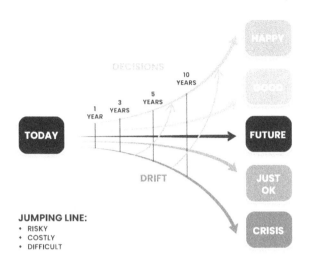

To jump lines is possible. But at the expense of time, money and increasing risk the longer you leave it. So, let's consider this:

Right now, at this very moment, is the closest you will ever be to your Happy Place line.

Right now.

Let that sink in.

So, when do you want to get started?

You know what your answer is, but I can tell you that the best answer is "today" because those lines you see in the graphic are curves and they compound. That means that the sooner you join the Happy line and put yourself on the path to success, the sooner you get to ride the curve and enjoy the positive impact of success. Remember, you don't just wake up one day and find that success has arrived. It's a gradual process where planning and discipline bring you success, compounding returns and wealth on your way to that Happy Place. So from a practical standpoint what does Happy actually look like? Remember the iceberg we discussed back in Chapter 1?

By following the outlines in this book, you can have:

1. Full visibility of your financial situation both today and into the future;
2. An optimised and planned investment strategy that is balanced to your future needs of expenditure and growth;
3. The ability to maximise your overall wealth by making all the right decisions at the right times.

Sounds pretty good doesn't it? But how is that all possible I hear you ask?

The good news is that the rest of this book will show you how to get onto that Happy line. I will show you a structure – or blueprint – for you to work through the three main areas of finance – Planning, Saving and Investing – with my help outlining the specific actions you need to take to get to you on the path to your Happy scenario. I will also show you how to stay on that path through regular check-ups and reviews that you can do yourself.

And if that is not enough, consider this. The further you go along that line, the more active decisions you take, the further you move away from the Crisis and Just OK scenarios. Think about it, you are not only increasing the likelihood of achieving your Happy scenario, you are at the same time reducing the likelihood of ending up in Crisis or Just OK. Sound good?

In the following chapters I'm going to unveil to you the Financial Blueprint – my system for financial success that I've built over years of being a financial planner and investment professional. The Financial Blueprint will give you nine specific actions to follow to give you full visibility of your finances, build an optimum investment strategy for you and overall maximise your wealth.

CHAPTER 5

Introducing the
Financial Blueprint

In this chapter you will learn

- *The powerful visual tool I use with all my clients*
- *The 9 steps that you will need to take to complete the blueprint*
- *How your own current situation stacks up and where you need to do the work*

One of the key skills of a good financial planner is to simplify thoughts to the most basic concept, yet still achieve the desired result. Over many years and thousands of conversations with clients and other individuals, I built up in my mind my perfect strategy for clients, my Blueprint if you like, that will help everyone achieve their desired financial success – or Happy Place.

I normally only share this with my clients, many of whom pay thousands of pounds to go through our full onboarding process. I have never published this Blueprint on any blog or newsletter or website because it is my intellectual capital, however I now feel this model is so powerful that it is worth sharing with everyone through this book.

The key with the Financial Blueprint is that it is a visual model. The reason for this is that the human mind is far better at thinking logically with pictures. "A picture is worth a thousand words" has never been truer, especially when trying to explain potentially complex topics and concepts with many different parts.

The concept of the model is that also it is interlocking and interdependent. It is almost impossible to achieve the ultimate outcomes without doing all the underlying specific tasks first. The good news however, is that each task is specific and I will show you how to do it.

Now remember back to Chapter 1 and the iceberg? How do most people think a financial plan should start? Most people – and frankly most financial planners – will say, "Well, first you should look at your investments, then your pensions etc., etc." Wrong! Your plan, your life should be all about achieving your Happy Place – remember this is a *Plan For Happy*. Every plan needs to start with the destination otherwise it is essentially useless and your money should be made and structured to help you achieve this – so this is where we begin.

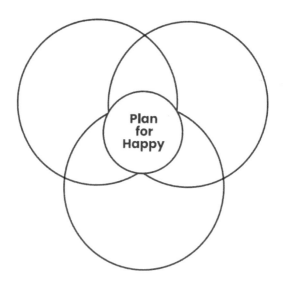

To get to that Happy Place we must achieve three main outcomes.

1. Full visibility of your financial situation today and in the future. You have to know where you are and where you're going.
2. An optimised investment strategy that is designed specifically for you, taking into account the split of your assets between long and short-term as well as your comfort level with risk and volatility.
3. Maximise your wealth, no matter what level you're starting at. To maximise your wealth we need to make sure that we are taking specific actions each year, no matter what markets are looking like, that are planned to be tax-efficient and all accumulate to build that long-term wealth.

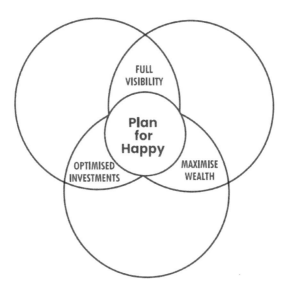

As the model begins to come together now you can see we arrive at the building blocks stage. To achieve the desired outcomes I mentioned above, we need to have the three basics of any good financial plan – Planning, Saving and Investing.

For most people, they don't have a financial plan and many live pay-cheque to pay-cheque. I don't need to explain any more how unsustainable that is for building wealth. Using this financial blueprint to build a detailed financial plan, my aim is to get you from a mess of papers to mastery of your finances.

Saving is really the crux of building any wealth as you cannot grow assets if you're spending all of them. By following our savings plan outlined in the rest of this book, I am looking to take you from profligate to prudent without taking the fun out of life.

And finally investing, making your money work hard for you and grow over time, can be perceived as risky and confusing. My role is to demystify investments and financial markets and show how you can use the concepts of time and risk to your advantage when investing. From clueless to confident in investing.

Now we have the basic blueprint in place. You can hopefully start to see how all the different factors work together to achieve the outcomes and ultimately towards our Happy Place.

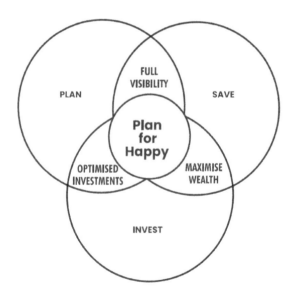

But we're not done yet.

For each of the building blocks – Plan, Save, Invest – there are three specific tasks or "accelerators" that I call them, that you need to do to achieve your outcomes. Don't worry, I will explain each clearly over the rest of the book – they each have a dedicated chapter – so you'll know exactly the steps to take and why you're doing it.

For the Plan, we are going to do the following:

1. Set goals.
2. Calculate trajectory.
3. Consider retirement.

When we are thinking about how to Save, we will:

1. Understand spending.
2. Start savings pots.
3. Increase monthly surplus.

And finally, thinking about how to Invest, we will:

1. Build knowledge.
2. Construct the investment strategy.
3. Put the plan into action.

This is your Financial Blueprint.

This is the map to achieving your financial Happy Place.

As you achieve each of the accelerators around the outside, you are getting closer and closer to achieving each outcome, which in turn works towards achieving the ultimate Happy Place. I would encourage you to print this page off (you can find a PDF on the website www.adamwalkom.com) and tick off each accelerator as you work around the blueprint.

How do you score today?

As an exercise to begin, look at each of these accelerators around the outside – all nine of them. Then consider where you are today for each of them and give yourself a ranking out of ten. Be honest with yourself. Let's go through them with a bit more explanation to help you score yourself honestly.

PLAN

1. Set goals – How clearly have you defined future goals? Do you know where your headed? Do you have short, medium and long-term goals in place?
2. Calculate trajectory – How do you know if you're on track for those goals? Do you keep a spreadsheet of investments and/or spending and income?
3. Consider retirement – How much have you thought about what your retirement looks like? Do have a strong idea of when and how you stop working? Or you may even not stop?

SAVE

1. Understand spending – How well do you know how much you spend each month or year? Have you split it out into categories? Do you know the difference between your discretionary and non-discretionary spending?
2. Start savings pots – Do you have savings pots set-up? Are they split out for different goals and/or scenarios? Do you have a rainy-day fund?
3. Increase monthly surplus – Have you thought about ways to increase your monthly surplus? Have you taken active steps to reduce your spending? Are you pursuing ideas to increase your income?

INVEST

1. Build knowledge – How is your knowledge of investment markets? Do you know what the key drivers of investment performance are for you? How comfortable are you with "risk" and do you think about how you can best use it for your situation?

2. Construct the investment strategy – Have you thought about your investment strategy? Have you split out the strategy into different timeline or goal scenarios? Do you take particular risks with different particular pots? Do you use low-cost index tracker funds?

3. Put the plan into action – Do you have an investment strategy in place? Have you consolidated your pensions into one easy-to-use place? Do you use your ISA allowance each year? Are you being tax effective with your pension? Do you use low-cost index tracker funds?

Remember, give yourself a score out of ten for each. Don't worry, nobody else needs to know. Now total up the scores.

If you scored anything >40: Amazing, you have a big head-start and are well on the way.

If you scored between 20 and 40: Great: There are already some positives there but there is lots of work to be done.

If you scored <20: Fantastic. Now you realise how valuable this Blueprint is in terms of improving your situation.

After finishing this book, there should be no reason why you wouldn't mark yourself 10 for each accelerator.

You will have a well-designed financial plan that builds towards your ultimate goal. You will have a detailed savings plan that will build your wealth in a relatively painless way and finally you will have a specific investment strategy, designed just for you.

Imagine how that feels? That feeling you had just then, that is your Happy Place. That is what we're aiming to achieve together.

Now, lets' get started.

CHAPTER 6

Setting Goals

In this chapter you will learn

- *How to split out your goals into certain time periods*
- *The importance of digging deeper and asking "why"*
- *The power of splitting goals into needs and wants*

Why do we even bother setting goals?

Simple answer: Because if we don't, how the hell do we know where we're headed?

More complex answer: Goal setting restructures your brain function to actually help achieve those goals. It's self-reinforcing.

A fascinating article on Inc.com,[10] highlights the following neurological reasons as to why goal-setting actually works. To put it in normal terms that you and I can understand they describe:

1. The part of your brain that creates emotion (your amygdala) evaluates the degree to which the goal is important to you.
2. The part of your brain that does problem solving (your frontal lobe) defines the specifics of what the goal entails.

---

10 https://www.inc.com/geoffrey-james/what-goal-setting-does-to-your-brain-why-its-spectacularly-effective.html

3. The amygdala and frontal lobe work together to keep you focused on, and moving toward, situations and behaviours that lead to the achievement of that goal, while simultaneously causing you to ignore and avoid situations and behaviours that don't.

Without getting into too much further science, let's think about this for ourselves in a totally unrelated concept. Let's say I want a chocolate biscuit. Without me consciously doing anything, my brain initially starts imagining the taste and sweetness of the biscuit and gives me a little dopamine – the pleasure hormone – hit to get me tempted. Then the problem-solving part kicks in and I ask, "How am I going to get a chocolate biscuit?" which involves the practicalities of opening the cupboard, taking out the tin etc., etc. Our brains process all this in milliseconds. At the same time, we are also considering the other questions around priorities and sacrifices. If I go and eat a chocolate biscuit, what else should I be doing in that time? Is that not more important? What about my health, sugar levels in my blood, fitness goals etc., etc. All of these tiny micro-decisions are made in a very short amount of time as we go about evaluating the goal of eating a chocolate biscuit and whether we are going to achieve it. See how this example works through the steps 1, 2 and 3 above?

As you can see from the above example we are setting goals every day, no matter how banal they may seem. Whether it be eating a chocolate biscuit or ticking off our to-do lists. Goals are part of our everyday life, so why does setting longer-term or financial goals feel more difficult? As soon as someone mentions the phrase "goal-setting" most normal people want to run away and hide. Yet, from a long-term happiness point of view, working towards achievable goals in itself increases happiness as pointed out by Dr Timothy Pychyl writing for *Psychology Today*.[11]

---

11 https://www.psychologytoday.com/gb/blog/dont-delay/200806/goal-progress-and-happiness

He also highlights how positive feedback from making progress towards our goals contribute further to our motivations to act. He describes "a win-win situation if we can just get started".

So let's get started. To do so, I'm going to make this easier for you.

We're going to break down the goals, into three sections: Short, medium and long-term.

And instead of thinking about the word "goals", we are going to consider needs and wants.

Good financial planners will talk to you about your goals and start mapping them out. Great financial planners will instead split it into needs and wants. This way we cover the needs or basics so you can at least have comfort you will have some level of existence. Think of this as protecting the downside somewhat. Then we consider also the aspirational side – the wants – instead of just what we need to happen, what do we want to happen? Note the small but important shift from just generic "goals" but this process gets us thinking more practically. You will see examples of this further along in the chapter.

For this exercise we should be writing these needs and wants down. There is significant scientific research which shows the simple act of physically writing things down means a) they tend to stay in our heads longer and b) we have more chance of achieving them.

There is an easy-to-use Needs and Wants PDF on my website at www.adamwalkom.com

As you go through this exercise, I want to you consider one very important word when coming up with the needs and wants. That word is "Why?". Why are these needs vital to me and my families' financial security? Why is this want on my list? What is it about it that means I want it?

To let you into one of my personal wants in the 10+ year bucket list is a large family home that I never have to sell. "The forever home" that my children remember and then come back to when they're older. Why is that a want for me? Well, as I described earlier, my parents sold our family home to put into their business and never got the chance to buy another one again. I don't want that happening to my children.

See how powerful that why question can be? Note how it also goes back to the emotional context of money that we discussed in Chapter 2. All of our needs and wants come from somewhere and my experience of working with hundreds of clients over the years, is that somewhere is something in each person's upbringing.

Make sure you do that for yourself. But please keep in mind that there is nothing to be ashamed of here as well. "I want to buy a Lamborghini" may not be on many people's list, but if that is a key want for your own sense of self-gratification, that's ok. Don't be ashamed, don't be embarrassed. By asking the why question, you will uncover the reasons behind these decisions and frankly, allows you to have much better internal justification for these decisions because you understand where they come from.

Having many varied goals

Back in Chapter 3 we discussed your Happy Place. You imagined and visualised your retirement goal – where you are and what you're going to be doing. But in life we have many other goals along the way. For some it's paying for the children's education, for some it's buying a bigger house, and for others it's getting debt free. It doesn't matter what it is; having the goal in the first place is what counts.

For this exercise: What are the most important things you need or want to do over the next 5, 10 or 20 years? You can download this PDF from adamwalkom.com. Each of these are targets around which we can tailor individual plans. I would normally sit down with my clients to do this, but because I can't be sitting there with you, I'm going to trust you'll do this on your own.

Write down on the PDF two or three key needs or wants you will want to use savings to pay for over the next 1–5 years.

So think short-term – what's on the horizon?

Do you want to move to a bigger house?

Do you have school fees to pay? A car loan to pay off? Be

completely debt free?

Be practical and make sure you split correctly between Need and Want. They are definitely not the same thing.

Key Needs & Wants Over Next 1–5 Years

Need	Want

Now write below two or three key needs or wants you will want over the next 5–14 years.

This is more medium-term. This time horizon potentially allows for career-changes, children finishing school and/or moving out, downsizing.

Key Needs & Wants Over Next 5–14 Years

Need	Want

And now, two or three key needs or wants for 15+ years (this should be similar to your Happy Place exercise from the previous chapter).

In this long-term, whilst also considering your Happy Place, try to think realistically about what you will actually need to survive and cover the basics.

Key Needs & Wants Over Next 15+ Years

Need	Want

Having established each of these needs and wants will help us build relevant savings pots and an investment plan that includes all of them. That's the magic of the Financial Blueprint – it's all inter-related and reliant on each other.

As we consider these needs and wants, we also need to consider the impact volatility has on our lives. Real life doesn't just happen in a straight line. So why do we create plans that pretend this is the case?

If you're having trouble coming up with needs and wants for the exercise above here is an idea.

One of the best ways to achieve this is to sit down with close friends or family or partners and start talking about the future and what you would like it to look like. Think of the good times, but also the challenges you may face along the way. The key to this discussion is that it has to come from your heart – it has to be really who "you" are. The you that has many different plans and goals and yet, like all of us, limited resources (specifically both money and time) to achieve them.

This is what real financial planning is. It's not what funds you're in and just whether you've used your ISA allowance for this year – though both of those can be important. It's having in-depth conversations about where you are and what you want your life to look like in 5, 10, 25 years and putting specific plans in place to achieve those goals.

To try to bring this to life, let me give you an example.

Recently I've created a plan for a client who is just coming up to her retirement. We considered the following different stages of this change of life moment:

These were her goals:

Short-term
Winding down full-time work, but considering part-time contracting.

Medium-term
Looking to spend early retirement travelling with her husband to see family overseas and lots of holidays.

Long-term

Concerned about inheritance tax in passing wealth down to children.

Note how we split them out into time-specific sections, however at this early stage of the conversation, the points highlighted above are very much generalist "goals". So we needed to go a little deeper, into needs and wants. As we continued our conversation, and I kept asking the "why?" question, the following came out of it.

These were the same goals split out into needs and wants:

Short-term

Need: To understand current pension provision and projected income if stopping work in two years with no follow-on work.

Wants: Pensions that allow funds to be drawn flexibly if required at any point.
Would actually like to keep working, so start networking now to line-up work and establish credibility.

Medium-term

Needs: Extra income over first five years of retirement to fulfil lifetime dream of living in France in Summer and US in winter.

Wants: Funds set aside to purchase house in France, potentially with interest only mortgage.

Long-term:

Needs: To ensure future income is protected against inflation.

Wants: To ensure wealth is protected against inheritance tax and have created gifting plan for children.

Note how we have drilled down deeper for each original goal. This allows much more specific targets set that both give the client a minimum of protection but also starts thinking about the further upside. A one-size-fits-all-everything-is-medium-risk approach simply cannot cover the specific needs for this client, or anyone for that matter.

Planning this way allows us to be far more specific in terms of the savings and investment plan. Using the framework above can begin to now set aside particular amounts, or "pots" as we'll call them in the next few chapters, that will work specifically for each need and/or want.

To go one step further on the example, below were the specific recommendations for that client. They were designed to cover off the need, but also practically work towards the want.

It looked something like this:

Short-term

Conducted full pension analysis and generated financial model for client. Consolidated multiple pensions into a flexi-drawdown scheme that is designed for medium-risk growth over the next five years which can then be drawn down as income once she has stopped work altogether.

Medium term

Switched funds in ISAs to cautious-risk income generating to provide tax-free income. Also planned to access small amounts of tax-free cash from pension depending on how much contracting income comes in. Plan to rent out UK property whilst abroad to create extra income.

Long-term

Maximise pension contributions over next few years whilst still working as pensions are outside of the estate for inheritance tax. Move pension strategy to 100% equity. Created discounted gift trust with lump sum to provide income today but also start seven-year clock ticking to remove funds from estate. As trust was invested for children to access in next 15–20 years, happy to take a more aggressive risk-approach.

Don't worry too much about the specific terms and actions above as we will cover all of those later in the book, but I wanted to give you an indication on how specific we can get on the actions around the plan.

Setting goals not only makes sense from a strategic perspective, it also works neurologically. The process itself forces us to think in different timelines about the future. It also allows us to split the goals into a baseline of what we need and an aspiration of what we want which is enormously valuable

In the following chapter we are going to work out how to see if we are on-track to achieve those targets and what we can do about it if we're not.

CHAPTER 7

Calculate Trajectory

In this chapter you will learn

- *How to do some basic calculations to establish where you are financially*
- *How to work out if you are on the right path*
- *To calculate the "big number", your retirement goal that you are working towards*

Having established needs and wants in the previous chapter was a great first step. This chapter takes that line of thinking further where we work backwards and calculate "the big number". This is your target retirement savings. This is how much you're going to need to have to live comfortably when you decide to stop working. Many people write this number down, stick it on the fridge, commit it to memory or somehow make this their burning target. We talked last chapter about the brain-hacking benefits of committing to targets and this is a prime example.

The process in this chapter involves some basic financial calculations which are not overly difficult, but do require a little bit of work. Let's get to work.

The first step is to get a rough idea on how much you spend in an average month. Amazingly, some people actually know this because they track/monitor on a spreadsheet. There are also useful bank accounts that help categorise your spending for you as well. If you don't, then don't worry as we will explore your spending habits further on in the Saving section of the book. For this calculation I'll make it easy.

Calculating monthly surplus and projected retirement income:

1. Think about what you have coming into your current account on a monthly basis. That is, the net pay for you, potentially your partner and/or any other income.
2. As the month ends think about roughly what is left over, if anything. If you're not sure just think, does your current account generally move up or down over the year? If up, then you've got a surplus, if down then you've got a shortage.
3. If you have £5k per month coming in and typically have around £500 left, then spending is £4,500. If you have £5k per month coming in and there is nothing left and in fact you continue to use around £1k other savings each month, then your spending probably is £6k per month.
4. Take the total figure of spending and remove costs that won't be there in say 20 years – that could be mortgage payments, school fees, car loan, life insurance etc. Also add back in any money that you are already contributing to savings or pensions. As an example, this could reduce spending £6k per month down to say £4k per month.
5. Multiply this figure by 12. This is your annual projected spending for when you retire.

On paper this looks to be a very simplistic measure, however don't let this fool you. It is precisely because it is simple it is so magical. For most people when you ask them what they want their retirement to look like, they will actually say is they want a life very similar to what they live today, just without the work. We are all creatures of habit. As we age we get used to a certain way of living with certain costs and we generally have in our minds an ideal plan to continue that standard of living into our retirement – hence using the same cost assumptions generally works as a rule of thumb. Think about that for a second. Is that correct for you?

The key to keeping this simple is not getting technical. Yes, inflation is currently a big issue, but far from a mathematical perspective we are just using the level of today's money across all the calculations so we offset any need for using inflation by doing this.

Back to our example, a couple spending £4k per month therefore needs around £48k per year to live in the future. Great – now we then need to gross this up for tax purposes, which means that £48k per year net spend, needs around £56k per year in income.

Now, your turn. Do it for your own situation. How did you get on? Completing this exercise will give you a good assumption of your basic income need in retirement. How does that number feel? Is it more or less than you thought it would be? Just by simply doing this calculation puts you ahead of 90% of the population (based on my experience) who simply have no idea and just trust "everything will turn out ok." I don't know about you, but that is not something I am prepared to accept.

All well and good you say, but where is this income going to come from?

We've only just started with the maths – we need to continue.

Now we're going to calculate the potential income you already will receive in retirement, and take it off the total income required. This leftover income is what we need to provide for. Make sense?

Calculating income

1 – State pension. As the rules are today at the time of writing, as long as someone has worked and made National Insurance (NI) contributions for 35 years over their lifetime, they will get the full state pension. Even if you haven't made the full 35 years, and worked say 32 years, then it is pro-rated so you get 32/35ths of the full state pension. Mothers who take time

off for children shouldn't worry either because as long as they receive child benefit they are receiving credit for NI contributions so they are not disadvantaged. The state pension also has the advantage of the triple-lock which means it will go up by the lower of 2.5%, Average Weekly Earnings growth, or Consumer Price Inflation (CPI).

Married or have a long-term partner? Even better. As long as you plan to stay together you both will receive the state pension.

At this point the full state pension is around £10,300 per year, but this will continue to increase over time.

Back to our example, for a couple who need £56k per year, this can contribute £20,600 towards that target, meaning there is around £35,400 left.

2 – Final salary or defined benefit pensions.

If you're lucky enough to have one of these pensions, then they will give you a projection on what you are likely to receive at retirement date. Minus that figure off your target.

3 – Rental and other non-work-related income.

Same as above for the other pensions. On the assumption this will continue into retirement, minus that off your target as well.

4 – Calculating savings target.

After you've set your initial projected income and now minused off the guaranteed income coming in, you should have a balance left over.

Using our example, let's say this is £30k per year. To calculate our savings target we simply multiply this figure by 25. So for the example this gives us a retirement savings target of £750k.

Why multiply by 25? This is using a well-known retirement calculation called "the 4% rule". The 4% rule suggests that if a retiree withdraws 4% off their retirement savings out each year then they are highly unlikely to run out of money. And 4% of £750k is, you guessed it, £30k per year.

There are many issues with the 4% rule, such as age of retirement, a big assumption on investment returns and the fact that spending slows down in your later years. When we sit with our clients, we go into far more detail with each of them around their own individual situation, however for this simplistic calculation it will suffice.

There you have it. When you think now, "How much will I need to save to retire to live the live I want to live?" This is the number.

This is the big figure you want to put on the wall as your retirement target. As I mentioned at the top of the chapter it may look like a big number, but now we have something concrete to aim for. A specific financial target for you.

You can do it.

Now we just need to work out how. With more maths. Starting today.

Let's work out where you are today and then we can work out what the future path looks like.

Step 1 – Add up all your savings, investments, pensions, crypto, whatever you have.

(Brief note on mortgages: I'll make the assumption here that if you have a mortgage it's on a repayment term. By having mortgage as a repayment mortgage, I'm assuming this debt just takes care of itself over the life of the mortgage. This clearly impacts monthly spending as it increases your expenditure, but normally it is well worth it as it takes away the worry about paying it off eventually. Bit by bit, you will get there with a repayment mortgage.)

Look at the total value that you have saved today and compare that to the final figure. I'm sure it looks like you've got a long way to go. Don't worry, it's the same for most people.

However, you have an advantage. You are about to learn a secret that is so fundamental to the world of finance and the broader world in general Albert Einstein called it "the eighth wonder of the world". Compounding.

Compounding is growth on growth. If something compounds at 7% for ten years in a row – it doubles. If you let it compound at 7% for 20 years – you make four times your original money. And what do you need to do? Simply not touch it! Leave it alone and let the market forces do the heavy lifting.

We will discuss the benefits of compounding and time in the market further in the Investment section of the book.

Step 2 – On our website (www.adamwalkom.com) we have built an easy-to-use compound calculator. Plug in your numbers, choose an interest rate (start using 7% to see how you get on) and length of years to your planned retirement. I will go into much more detail on what figure to use in later parts of the book. For the sake of the exercise – and reality – you should choose somewhere between 2% and 9% for this figure. The lower the number, the more conservative you are being on the growth prospects, the greater likelihood you will achieve that number.

Take a look at the final projected number after you input the growth rate. If your current savings level achieves the final retirement figure without any more contributions – fantastic. You are there. You have built up enough assets to have a sustainable retirement based on the expenses we've estimated – congratulations. Now your work is just don't mess it up!

However if you are like most people, there is more work to do. Most people will continue to need to put money away into savings, investments and pensions for the rest of their working life. There is nothing wrong with that. Don't worry about the precision of this target because it is only a rough estimate.

Being precise about the amount you need to put away per month at the moment is pointless – and frankly can be depressing. Incomes change, events happen, inheritances arrive and other non-planned events impact everybody's lives over a 20+ period. There is no point getting hung up on exact amounts so early on. The Savings section will look in detail at what you can put away and also give you a plan on how to maximise that figure.

There we have it. We have a target and we have a projected growth path for you at this point without any more additions to your savings. The gap between those figures may look large now, but the entire principle of the rest of this book is reducing that gap in a planned, controlled way that makes it feel managed and hopefully even easy!

CHAPTER 8

Planning Retirement

In this chapter you will learn

- *About the modern world of retirement and how it has changed since our grandparents*
- *The significant benefits of staying in work*
- *How to think about how much to draw out*

What actually is retirement?
We all probably have an inner view of what it looks like to be retired and if you're like me it brings to mind the image of my grandparents when I was younger.

The fact is though what they knew as retirement and what we will know as retirement will probably be very different experiences.

Working until your 60 in one company, the gold watch on retirement, final salary pension, then retirement days spent doing a combination of cruises and golf clubs. Fairly safe to say that those days are gone.

Whilst some people may lament that idea, many would say the flexibility and options we have in retirement now vastly improve the quality of life for the older generations.

How our retirement world will look different from our grandparents' world.

Average Years in Retirement (UK)

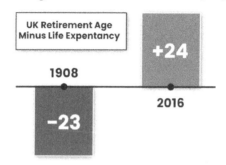

As the chart above shows, at the start of the 20th century, the average person in Britain could expect to die 23 years before they retired. Yes, I know that's ridiculous; the point I'm making is that life expectancy was such that the average person died 23 years before they reached the age at which those brand-new state old age pensions became payable. Life expectancy now is such that the average person can expect to live at least 24 years *after* they reach retirement age – 24 years that deserves a little planning, because if you get it right they could be the happiest 2½ decades of your life.

Ageing around the globe: a greying population 2015-2050

Source: Transforming World Atlas, Bank of America Merill Lynch, July 2018.

This chart shows how the age of the population around the world looked seven years ago. The closer the colour gets to orange and red, the higher the percentage of the population aged 65 and above. Look at this chart and it seems that only Japan has anything at all to worry about. But now let's fast-forward to 30 years from now:

Source: Transforming World Atlas, Bank of America Merill Lynch, July 2018.

Most of Africa still looks young, and so do parts of Asia and South America, but overall the world is ageing. The good thing about that from the point of view of anyone planning their retirement is that the "grey vote" will grow in importance and issues concerning the elderly will get more attention. In a more negative vein, there are going to be far more people relying on the capital they have accumulated to get them through their retirement years.

Let's look at that a little more closely. This next chart takes the USA as a proxy for the Western world and asks the question: What percentage of the population aged 55 and over is actively engaged in work?

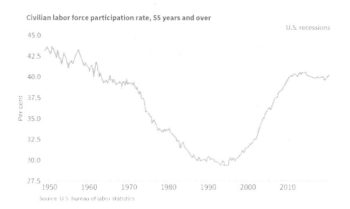

Civilian labor force participation rate, 55 years and over

Source: U.S. bureau of labor statistics

These are official figures and so, as official figures do, they exclude the considerable number of people aged 55 and over who are fully engaged in looking after grandchildren or caring for partners. Be that as it may, some 40% of people aged 55 and over are working and the line marking those figures is likely to continue to move higher as retirement ages everywhere increase.

The next chart reflects the way that received ideas about how a 'normal' life (whatever that may be) is lived:

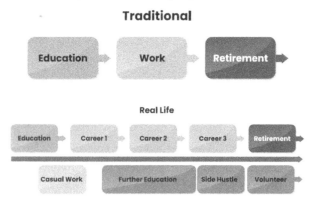

The "Traditional" diagram illustrates the idea that persists everywhere about life going through many stages. A "real" life does not pass through three clearly defined and separated stages;

you can be in more than one stage at the same time, you can move backwards as well as forwards (and you can even move sideways) and, perhaps most significantly of all, you have to take care of your movement through the stages yourself. The welfare state is a wonderful thing and it has improved the lives of many, but it has had at least one unfortunate consequence: it has led people to believe that there will always be someone else to step in when things are tough. Some authority figure who will say, "Don't you worry about that. I'll take care of that for you." It won't happen. Taxpayers would have to pay and taxpayers can't afford it.

The concept of portfolio work and different careers highlighted in the graphic above sounds a little complex, so I define this as simply continuing to work in some way, shape or form post full-time work. Post covid-lockdown labour shortages and the rise of flexible working practices has increased enormously, and this has been a boon to the older worker. The ability to work remotely has now been fully accepted and almost expected by most employees and employers. Less travel, more varied employment options, flexible time options are some of the many benefits of flexible working that suit the older worker. And that is before we get to the health benefits as well.

The benefits of working older is also backed up by the scientific research.

A 2016 study of 3,000 people suggested that working even one more year beyond retirement age was associated with a 9% to 11% lower risk of dying during the 18-year study period, regardless of health.[12]

Also, a 2015 study of 83,000 older adults over 15 years suggested that, compared with people who retired, people who worked past age 65 were about three times more likely to report being in good health and about half as likely to have serious health problems, such as cancer or heart disease.[13]

---

12 https://www.health.harvard.edu/staying-healthy/working-later-in-life-can-pay-off-in-more-than-just-income
13 https://www.health.harvard.edu/staying-healthy/working-later-in-life-can-pay-off-in-more-than-just-income

Other studies have linked working past retirement age with a reduced risk of dementia and heart attack.

The most obvious avenue for working into older age is through knowledge-based work – you simply need decent Wi-Fi and a laptop – but even some of the manual trade industries are utilising older workers so they can tap their experience. The Construction Industry Council (CIC) published an article titled "Older workers crucial to curbing construction industry skills gap".[14] After completing a survey of nearly 1,000 members they found the financial benefits of continuing to work are significant.

The first is obvious which is the income you've got coming in can help pay monthly bills, reducing the amount you need to draw out of your retirement savings and helping them last longer. If you can earn enough to cover the day-to-day bills for five years without drawing down, that's five more years the pot has to increase in value so that when you do call on it, you're calling on a bigger sum. Think back to our discussion on compounding. A larger sum, growing at the same growth rate, produces a larger return. Keep going for ten years and the benefit is even bigger. And all of that affects the final decision we are working towards which is: What percentage of your retirement pot should you draw down annually to be certain that it won't run out of steam before you do? That, in other words, you won't run out of money in the later years of your retirement.

How to think about what income you can draw.

Before 2014 your retirement income options were rather restricted. Either you had a final salary (also called defined benefit) pension which was given to you by your employer or you had built up your own private pension pot and you were forced to buy an annuity with it.

An annuity is simply a guaranteed pension income. To buy an annuity you would sell your pension pot to an insurance company who guaranteed to pay you a certain income (it could

---

14 https://www.cic.org.uk/news/older-workers-crucial-to-curbing-construction-industry-skills-gap?s=2015-12-09-older-workers-crucial-to-curbing-construction-industry-skills-gap

be flat or linked to inflation) for the rest of your life.

The regulator loves annuities because they provide a stable, guaranteed income and don't allow you to alter them at all once they have been set-up. Unfortunately, just because the regulator likes them it doesn't mean it's the best outcome for each individual.

In 2015 the then Chancellor, George Osborne, introduced what was described as "pension freedoms". These freedoms gave the individual total freedom in terms of how you take your pension income. In short, you can access your pension at any point over 55 years old, and you get the first 25% tax-free, whilst the balanced is taxed at your marginal rate at the time you draw it.

Offering this flexibility was a fantastic result for individuals who now have total freedom in terms of how they draw their pension. The problem though is this freedom can be confusing. Individuals don't always make the most sensible decisions. The wisest financial decision is not always the most obvious. The need for advice jumped significantly at this point.

Going further than the 4% rule
In the calculation section we looked at multiplying our potential retirement income by 25 to give us the total amount required – this referenced the 4% income drawdown rule and I highlighted how simplistic this measure was. We're going to explore this concept further now using something called probabilistic thinking.

When it comes to deciding how much of your pot you can afford to draw down each year without risking running out of money, it would be very easy to simply give up in the face of all the things we don't know. You don't know how many years you have left. You don't know (and, if you do, please tell me because I certainly don't know) what the future holds in the way of inflation, tax regimes and return on investments. So let's think about how we can arrive at the closest possible estimation of what may lie in wait for us. How do we do that? We look at the past.

Probabilistic thinking is a way of arriving at a working solution when we don't have all the facts. What it says is: We can't be certain, but if we take into account what has happened in the past and the best idea we have of what may happen in the future, it is most likely that things will turn out this way. It might be slightly out, but chances are this will be the result we see.

There has been a lot of work using probabilistic thinking to decide what percentage of a retirement pot we can drawdown each year without risking emptying the pot while we are still alive. The first thing to decide is: how many years do you want to base your probability on? You could look at what typically happens over a period of 20 years, 30 years, 40 years or more. You could also look at any intervening period, like 24 years or 38 years. We are talking about probability here, so one of the things you might want to take into account is the probable maximum number of years you'll spend in retirement. If you expect to retire at sometime between, say, 55 and 65, 20 years is probably too short, while 40 years may well be too long, especially if you're a man (the number of women over 90 in the UK is double the number of men): as at 2019, only .01% of the UK population was over 90 years old and only 2% of those few made it past the 100-year mark (Estimates of the very old, including centenarians, UK – Office for National Statistics, 2020.) So taking rolling periods of 30 years between 1900 and 2017 may be the best approach, and that's convenient because the calculations have already been done for us. Overall, the conclusions are:

- Drawing down 3.5% of the pot each year would have left money in the pot at the end of the person's life in 90% of cases during the years 1900 to 2017[15]
- Drawing down 5% of the pot each year would have left money in the pot at the end of the person's life in 70% of cases.

And that's the sort of figure we have to work with. Remember, though, that these are long-term projections and, as we know, the funds in which the money is invested can drop suddenly for

---

15 Permanent Wealth Partners analysis

a relatively short time. You don't want to be drawing down from the pot during one of those years, and so the wise course of action is to have some of the pot in cash or cash equivalent. Then, when the funds have taken a sudden drop, you have recourse to the cash pot. How much should that cash pot be? That depends on your own levels of pessimism and optimism, but two years of drawdown may be a good place to start.

What this tells us is that nine out of ten people will never run out of money if they draw down 3.5% of their retirement pot each year and seven out of ten will be fine drawing out 5%. Let's also remember that these are percentages. If you have £1 million in your pension pot, 5% would be £50,000 each year and 3.5% would be £35,000 each year. You may need all of that to live the life you want to live – and you may not. If your joint state pension is £20,000 a year, you are earning another £10,000 a year from post-retirement work and you have a work pension of £12,000 a year, do you actually need another £50,000? Do you even need £35,000? It's different for everyone.

A worked example

Most of this book is focused on building up wealth. But there is just as much importance, if not more, in designing a strategy that draws down the wealth in the most tax-efficient manner. Paying an extra £2,000 of tax every year on a £40,000 income is equivalent to giving away 5% of your income every year to the taxman – surely a very good definition of madness.

When choosing how to withdraw funds, we discussed in the previous section the amount to draw down. That's up to you and I hope I've given you a good guide to what is reasonable. However, your choice of sources to take your income from makes a big difference.

Let's use a relatively common example. I will explain a scenario here, which will be typical for some people; if it doesn't describe your situation there are still likely to be parts of it that resonate.

Example:

I want to introduce you to Tom and Sally Smith. Tom is 65 years old and newly retired. He doesn't want to work part-time, but Mrs Sally Smith (also 65) still does and earns £8,000 per year in a part-time job which she plans to go on doing for the next few years.

They have an investment property which is mortgage free and pays them £10,000 per year in rental income, Tom has a final salary pension worth £15,000 per year (indexed). Sally Smith has a pension pot worth £200,000 and they have investment ISAs worth £100,000. They both should start receiving their full state pensions at age 67. Let's say they need £45,000 per year to live on. Ok, so what is the best way to draw their funds?

When no more income comes in, we need to think about two main priorities: 1) protecting the income against tax and 2) protecting the overall wealth against inflation.

Let's start with protection against income tax. This is all about making sure we use the personal allowances for both Tom and Sally sensibly. The personal allowance, on which you do not pay tax, is (in tax year 2022/23) the first £12,500 of your taxable income.

This is how Tom and Sally could split out their income:

Tom
£15,000 final salary pension
£5,000 rental income
£5,000 income from investment ISAs

Sally
£8,000 earnings
£5,000 rental income
£7,000 in tax-free cash from her pension

The rental income is split between them and takes Sally above her personal allowance so that she starts paying tax. Income withdrawn from ISAs is always tax-free, so we give that to Tom and then Sally can withdraw up to 25% of her pension pot (25% of £200,000 is £50,000) tax-free so we will choose to start withdrawing some of that.

This generates the £45,000 income required for the couple. Normally if one working person is paid £45,000 per year, they will pay £6,498 in tax. With the above combination, the total tax paid for Tom (£2,500) and Sally (£100) is just £2,600. A whopping £3,900 difference every year.

The advice on what to draw for Tom and Sally would change in a few years when their state pension starts, but it would be a similar type of saving.

Can you see how powerful this is?

Seeking professional financial help is always a good idea when it comes to your finances. When it comes to calculating how much income to draw out, I would suggest it is vital.

CHAPTER 9

The Psychology of Spending

In this chapter you will learn

- *How tracking your spending is the first step towards financial success*
- *Warren Buffett's best investment strategy*
- *How to play the "How much can I save today?" game*

What is wrong with the following picture?

John Brown is a 40-year-old management consultant on about £100,000 p.a. He is married, has two children and a reasonable mortgage. He doesn't feel under any particular financial pressure and, though he never has any money left at the end of the month, he feels that he and his family are living a decent sort of life. He isn't saving anything, but he says he will. One day. When he has enough. When his salary has gone up a little more. Sometimes, that idea is challenged a little when he remembers that he also felt his life was okay and he didn't have any money left at the end of the month when he was on £75,000 p.a. And, if it comes to that, things were much the same when his salary was £50,000 p.a. But things will change as soon as he is earning a little more. Of course they will.

But will they? No, they almost certainly won't, because there's one question that James can't answer and that question is: What did you spend your money on this month? What did you spend it on last month? Where, in fact, does your money go?

He knows about the big things. He and his wife have their own bank accounts and they also have a joint account which they call the housekeeping account; he pays £450 into that every month as soon as his salary arrives and they use it for grocery shopping. On the 25th of every month, the bank takes their mortgage payment from his account and it's also his account from which the house insurance, council tax and utility bills are paid. That's the agreement they have because, the children being the age they are right now, his wife only works three half days each week, so her income is just about enough to keep her in cover costs.

Even when those payments are made, John still has nearly £300 left. When the next payday rolls round, though, he's just about skint. Then the whole process starts again.

So, what happened to that £300? He's never really thought about it.

John's story above may sound very familiar to you. In fact, it sounds very familiar to me as I was John Brown. That story is based on my life before I became a financial planner. And trust me, if I can change, then I'm certain you can as well.

But let's got back to John for a second – on reflection, what is the biggest mistake John/I made in all those decisions above? Not sure? Clue: It's the final line.

He's never really thought about it.

The simple act of thinking about and trying to understand where you spending goes on a daily, weekly and yearly basis is the key first step you can make.

Before we get into the practical understanding of how you spend, let's understand ourselves on the why.

Why do you spend?

It's not that simple to say "Are you a spender or a saver?" – however identifying the financial influences of your past and upbringing will at least get you closer to understanding how you spend today, which in turn gives you the best chance to follow the best path.

The best example I'm going to give you is me. Given my rather volatile financial upbringing I have already discussed, you would think I would be a complete spendthrift? Well, not at all. My spending habits tend to be rather lumpy, but certainly sometimes I don't hold back. I spent my 20s quite happy to spend all my income as I was earning well in a large bank and it wasn't until really my family came along that I realised I needed to think about some sort of discipline around spending. You may be the same or you may be the other way around.

From experience of working with my clients, those that grew up with a certain level of income and therefore spending habits, find it very hard to reduce those. There is a classic quote, I have no idea where it is from but it's very true, about flying business class versus flying in economy. It is "once you turn left, it is very hard to turn back." The meaning being, flying business class is actually really, really nice. Once you experience it, then fly economy again, you know what goes on behind that little curtain and therefore the relative experience for you becomes worse. First-world problem I know, but this is how the human brain functions. If you recognise this in yourself, then you've most likely learned to spend, as we all know there are many opportunities, but now is the time to take some control of this.

If the answer is no, then my assumption would be you're more of a careful spender and putting the next chapter's savings plan is actually going to free up money for you to spend.

I have a fantastic client who recently retired with over £1.5 million in the bank. Great for him. So how does he want to spend it? He doesn't! He simply wants to continue to receive the same amount per month that he was whilst he worked – which was around £35 k per year. Why, you ask? We are all creatures of habit. If you are used to a certain lifestyle, then it feels odd to try to change that too much. I'm forever telling this client that he can afford to fly at the front of the plane on holiday, but he refuses to "What is the point?" he tells me. "You don't get there any faster!"

The danger comes from people who were well off at one point and now find themselves in a different situation. Life is never linear as we all know, so this situation is surprisingly common.

Many people in this situation struggle to adjust their spending habits lower because, internally for them, it feels as though they've been downgraded. The good news I have if this sounds familiar to you, is by following an automated saving strategy that I'm going to show you, you can remove the constant tricky decision-making element out of this which should make life much easier.

Understanding your spending

What do you spend your money on? If you're like most people, you can't give an accurate answer to that question. Money just tends to go. And the more you earn the more you tend to spend. There is no doubt that for most people our lifestyle grows to match our income. Think about the last time you got a pay rise. Did you put all of that money away into a savings and/or investment account? I bet you didn't, and you know why you didn't? Because you're human. Because you're normal. Because saving money is hard and spending a little more each money is much easier.

There's no huge mystery about where that money goes. It happens to us all. From time to time, my wife and I may go out for dinner. There's the cost of the meal and we have to pay a babysitter. Sometimes, instead of just the two of us, it's a family meal in the local pizza place. Occasionally, I will buy a bottle of wine to enjoy that weekend. Once in a while, there will be a movie that the kids want to see and what could be nicer than to stop at Pizza Express before we get back in the car to go home? And so it goes, and I have no doubt that you could write a similar list of things to spend money on. Those things are treats and treats are very important in all families and in all lives. If your plan doesn't include the occasional treat, you will never stick with it because keeping to an investment plan requires discipline and discipline is very hard to impose on yourself if you don't have the occasional relieving treat.

Typically most families don't have these treats as part of a plan. Instead, what people do is what I used to do. They think about going out for a meal, or think about responding to the children's request for a trip to the movies, and ask themselves if they have enough money at that point in the account. And, if they do, they go.

This was always a problem, even in our grandparents' day, but it's worse now because we have credit cards. A debit card isn't a problem because it's governed by the amount of money you have in your account and how far the bank is prepared to see you overdraw that account, and the old-style American Express cards also weren't a problem because Amex expected you to repay the full amount every month. You could have almost anything you wanted, as long as you could afford it – but you'd better be able to pay when your American Express statement arrived. With the kind of credit card we have now though, it's only too easy to give in to immediate desires and then find that you're stuck with a debt that has to be repaid and an interest rate that sucks up money you could otherwise have spent on another treat.

Or invested for the future.

Warren Buffet, investor extraordinaire, said in 2020 that a friend had come into some money and asked him what she should invest it in. He asked if she owed anything on credit cards; she did, and the interest rate was 18%. Buffet told her to pay off her credit card debt. He told a Berkshire Hathaway shareholders' meeting, "It's going to be way better than any investment idea I've got. She would save more money on interest than any return she could get by investing the money, whether in the stock market or in real estate or elsewhere. I don't know how to make 18%."[16] And neither do I.

So what should we do?

Discipline equals freedom

He – and you – should bring discretionary spending inside the plan. Food is not discretionary. You have to eat. The mortgage

---

16 https://www.cnbc.com/2020/05/13/warren-buffett-cautions-against-carrying-a-credit-card-balance.html

is not discretionary. You need a roof over your head. House insurance, utility bills – not discretionary. They have to be paid.

But those treats mentioned above are the very definition of discretionary spending. You don't have to have them, but if you allow yourself no treats at all then life will feel not worth living. So, when you make your plan, you include an allowance for treats. Having the plan means you can have the treats. This is what is meant by "discipline equals freedom". Why is this so important?

Former U.S Navy SEAL turned podcast host and author Jocko Willink describes discipline like this "The root of all good qualities. The driver of daily execution. The core principle that overcomes laziness and lethargy and excuses. Discipline defeats the infinite excuses that say: Not today, not now, I need a rest, I will do it tomorrow."[17]

Discipline by itself feels like hard work for good reason – it is. However, discipline with a goal in mind makes those tough actions easier. Think of the Happy Place. That's your why. The more vividly you can see that Happy Place, the easier the journey becomes, because the small sacrifices become worth something. They have meaning.

And by doing this, you trick your brain as well. With a strong, clearly defined long-term goal, saving becomes almost a game. Every time you feel you sacrifice some sort of discretionary spending think of this as a little win for you that should be celebrated. Think of it like a potential debit from your spending instead becoming a credit towards your goal. Once you establish this in your mind it is very powerful and becomes more like a game. "How much can I save today?" is a great mantra and then make sure you monitor the daily totals to give yourself that positive feedback.

But you don't just get there by little mental tricks alone. It takes time, it takes courage and it takes discipline to put the financial planning in place. But if it means you get to the Happy

---

17 Willink, Jocko *Discipline Equals Freedom: Field Manual*, St Martin's Press, p. 3

Place, is it worth it? I think you'll agree when you're there that it was. Because this is freedom.

That's what I'm trying to achieve with you throughout this book.

Freedom to retire and live how you want.

Freedom to spend time with loved ones on holidays or doing fun things because your finances allow it.

Freedom to have the reassurance that if bad things happen, your loved ones are protected.

Freedom to ignore all the doomsayers telling you every day how the market is going to crash.

Sound good? Now let's go do it.

CHAPTER 10

Building your Savings Plan

In this chapter you will learn

- *What it is you actually spend your money on*
- *To start building your savings plan*
- *How to work out your Rainy Day pot*

All self-help finance books seem to contain a similar unrealistic message: Put as much away as you can each month, whilst having complete foresight of all the ups & downs you may face in the future when you need cash.

Oh, if only it were that easy.

Why this book is different is because it gives you a system. A system which has the amounts calibrated based on your specific situation. A system that has been designed and tested by me over the last 20 years which not only has savings pots, but includes spending pots as well.

Recognising your spending habits

Before then you really do need to find out where your money is going because, as my old marketing professor taught me, "What gets measured gets managed, and if you can't measure it, you sure as hell can't manage it."

There are various ways to get a handle on your spending. I found it useful to switch my bank account to one of the modern online banks that have popped up in the last few years – like Monzo or Revolut or Starling. What I find useful about these banks is the way their app divides up what I spend and tells me where the money has gone. You could achieve the same result using a spreadsheet; the difference is that the online banks record every penny you spend (and where it goes) when you spend it and, if you use a spreadsheet, you have to remember to update it. It's very easy at the end of a month to find that you've accounted for most of the money you earned – but there's still £100 or so that you don't know where it went. For this to work properly, you really do need to know the fate of every penny.

Whichever way you go, try this activity. Look back at your spending from the last month and see where the money has gone. Any surprises there? I bet there are. Now go further. Look back at the last three months and then you should have a fairly accurate idea of what you're doing with your money. If you take the totals for each spending category for the last three months, then divide them by three – this helps smooth out the one-off hits that we constantly get. (As to why we lie to ourselves and continue to call these "one-off" hits is a story for another time.)

The categories of your spending should look something like this.

Fixed expenses:
Housing – rent or mortgage
Debt payments – car, credit cards
Utility payments – gas, electricity, phone, internet, gym membership
Transport – car, public transport fares
Groceries – food, personal care items
Discretionary expenses:
Entertainment – eating out, coffees out, Netflix, cinema etc.
Holidays
Clothes/shoes

The fixed expenses are exactly that. They're fixed and there is not normally much that can be done other than seeking cheaper shopping or riding a bike more often.

It is the discretionary expenses that we really want to focus on, this is where we can really make a difference. You now have a figure in front of you of how much you spend on discretionary, non-urgent items each month. Before we go on, please note how you're feeling at this point. If there is some sort of sick feeling or guilt as you look at your discretionary spending habits then contrary to how it may feel that is a good thing. You are identifying these habits and shining a light on them. There is no need to be embarrassed as think of it this way… you are now taking control of your own habits instead of allowing powerful marketing companies to hijack them! Because that is what they do.

We're just going to leave this figure as it is for now. Next chapter I will show you how to reduce it, but for now let's leave it as it is.

Before you think I'm going to say all discretionary spending is bad, hear me out. Discretionary spending is actually vital. It's what makes us, it defines who we are as a person in terms of the choices we make with our money. It makes us happy. I'll say it again to emphasise the importance. Spending money on treats makes us happy. What is money but numbers on a screen that allows us to live the life and express ourselves how we want to?

Not expecting that? Good. That's why what I'm about to show you is so powerful. A savings system that also lets you spend on treats. The system below not only automates your savings plan, but also creates the financial space for you to continue to express yourself with your money and buy those treats. The key word I've used above is "system" as having a system in place makes it easier for our brains not to have to think about it constantly. A recent study by the American Marketing Association on saving found some interesting results. They found that with an automated system, people on lower incomes tended to save at a higher rate than those on higher incomes, but the level very much depended on what they described as the persons "savings orientation".[18] In simple terms, this means if people actually wanted to save. There is no point in having a savings plan, if you don't have a specific goal to save for and the research from the previously mentioned study supports that. However, the flipside is also true. Having specific goals and targets for your saving plan, helps increase the success rate. It was reassuring to read this as I have come to the same conclusion, just through experience and years of doing exactly this. So combining both automation of savings, as well as specific savings goals, gives us the best possible success and this is exactly what I've done below in creating my savings system. I call it the Four-Headed Hydra.

The Four-Headed Hydra is based on the Greek mythological monster called the Hydra – a snake-like creature with four heads. Apart from the obvious deadly capability in having four sets of deadly fangs, the most famous aspect of the Hydra was its ability to regenerate one, even sometimes two, heads every time a warrior cut off one of its heads. This makes it effectively unkillable. This regeneration part is the vital component of every good plan, because there is no point having a plan that is fixed. Every plan needs to be flexible, needs to have the ability to regenerate as new and/or different situations occur that require a shift. And also because a Hydra looks pretty cool.

---

18 Newmeyer, C., Warmath, D., O'Connor, G. E., & Wong, N. (2021). Is Savings Automation Helpful to Liquid Savings? It Depends on Whether You Have a Savings Habit. *Journal of Public Policy & Marketing*, 40(2), 285–297. https://doi.org/10.1177/0743915620950216

Building your Four-Headed Hydra

Just like the Four-Headed Hydra we are going to establish four different savings pots through your online bank. You can think of them as savings pots, you can think of them as buckets, it really doesn't matter. What does matter is that you know that the money you earn is going to be divided right at the outset through automation into different pots. Some of those pots will be for savings, one of those pots will be for spending. We will get to the sums involved and how to do it later in the chapter. First step though is to set them up.

Pots that may look like this:

- Rainy Day pot
- Goal 1 pot (don't name it this, title it what you are actually saving for)
- Goal 2 pot (same for this)
- Treats

The purpose of the Rainy Day pot is obvious: You want to have some money saved for that broken boiler or the unexpected need to travel for a family emergency. You will establish in your own mind the right sort of amount to have in the Rainy Day pot; when you get there, you can stop allocating money to it each month until some of it has been spent though you should evaluate the amount from time to time and make sure it's still sufficient – we will go through how to calculate this figure shortly.

Goal 1 and Goal 2 are things that I want you to think about saving for over the next 1–5 years. One could be a two-year goal, the other could be a five-year goal. Does this sound familiar? Remember when in the previous chapter you wrote down your Key Needs and Wants over the next five years? This is where you use these. The important thing is to prioritise, so I'm asking you only to choose those that are most important to you. The important thing is to write them down. Examples could be: a new bike, an overseas holiday, a deposit for a flat. The important part is that it should be something substantial and something that will give you great pleasure in buying. Think about how you will feel when you have achieved those goals. Remember this feeling, because reminding yourself of this feeling will help control those spending impulses every month.

Decide what you are saving for over two years and over five years and make these things the names of the two pots. So, for example, the Goal 1 pot could be renamed New York Holiday pot and Goal 2 pot could be School Fees pot. Doing that reminds you each month of exactly why you are putting this money aside.

The key point about the Treats pot

Before we move on, let's be quite sure we understand the most significant point about that Treats pot. It's there because you need it. If you try to live a life completely without treats, then either your marriage or your financial planning will break apart. Treats are essential. But the amount you put into the Treats pot is the maximum amount you can spend. Once it's gone, it's gone and it doesn't matter how much you have available in cash – that belongs to your other pots. It's our old friend, having your cake and eating it: once you've eaten your cake, there will be no more cake until next month when you have filled the Treats pot again. Remember discipline equals freedom.

Calculating how much you can save

Okay – we're really making progress. We've set up the Rainy Day pot, allocated the specific Goals 1 & 2 to the savings pots and identified a Treat pot. But how much should you be putting away each month in your various pots? The simplest way to work this out is to look at how much comes into the account and take away the essential cost of living and the reduced budget on the three discretionary spending areas (entertainment, eating out and shopping). We did this earlier in the chapter where we looked at the average for each of the last three months spending.

Example: Income of £2,600 net per month
Minus fixed expenses £1,800 per month
Minus discretionary expenses budget £500 per month
Equals monthly surplus of £300 per month.

We will look at the next chapter at ways to increase that monthly surplus, so these figures that we set you up with can and most likely will change over time.

Start with the Rainy Day pot

The most important pot to start with is the Rainy Day pot. Nobody's spending is exactly the same month in, month out, so we need to have a safety net in place in case of overshoots and unexpected expenses. The best place for that is a Rainy Day pot.

The key question is: How large should this be? Some people choose three months income while others prefer six or even twelve months. It doesn't matter. The question I believe you need to answer is: When you wake up in the middle of the night, what would be the minimum balance of your cash savings that would enable you to go back to sleep?

So for the first three to six months – your choice – your goal is to put 100% of your monthly surplus into your Rainy Day pot.

Write down your Rainy Day pot target amount. That figure is your first goal.

My Rainy Day pot target is:

Key action: Direct all savings into just the Rainy Day pot until it gets to the level that you want it to be.

This is a good place to start as not only does it get you used to the discipline of saving but it also means the Rainy Day fund is easily accessible if you've overestimated your monthly surplus. And now you've begun! Over the next few months, really enjoy the look of that Rainy Day pot building up as you know you're taking steps to protect your financial future.

Bear in mind that, when you encounter a rainy day and have to spend some of your Rainy Day fund, you have to replace it. But don't worry. That's part of the plan and we reset our strategy at that point – just like cutting the head off the Hydra – one grows back in its place. That is what it is there for and the pot has done its job. It has also meant you haven't needed to access investment money that should be allowed to continue to grow over time without interruption. So if you do find yourself in a situation where you need to access your Rainy Day pot, pause the other savings plans for the short-term to rebuild the Rainy Day pot back up to the level

Moving on from the Rainy Day pot

Let's jump forward six months.

You've achieved your Rainy Day goal! Congratulations! Now we can get a little more proactive with building the future financial plan using the pots we have.

Because you've achieved your Rainy Day pot, we're just going to leave that there and not make any more contributions until we've had to draw some out to meet a sudden cost. Pot secured. By now, your budget should be working well and you should be a lot more comfortable with the amount you're spending and how it impacts you.

Now we can switch the monthly surplus over to split between the three other pots.

Goal 1 (written down previously)

Goal 2 (written down previously)

Treats

Going back to our monthly surplus figure of £300 per month. That may not sound like very much in one month, but if you can keep that up over five years, that will equal £18,000. And that is before you get any investment return on it.

If we used £300 per month and split evenly across Goal 1, Goal 2 and Treats, then we would spend the £100 per month on treats and save £200 per month across the two goals – leaving them with a potential balance of £6,000 each – plus any investment growth.

The split is totally up to you. And there we are – our short-term goals are set up. We know where we are going for the next five years. Humans have a great tendency to overestimate the amount they can achieve in a short-term timeframe but underestimate how much we can achieve given a much longer time horizon.

Where's the money coming from?

Many people will look at this and think, "Hang on, it would be nice to do all that but I simply don't have the money to spare." That's true for a lot of people – but it doesn't have to be.

To break away from the usual finance self-help books, I'm going to let you in on a few secrets. As already established, your monthly surplus is your income minus expenditure. There are two ways to increase that surplus – reduce the expenditure or increase the income. I'm going to show you a few options of how to do either or both.

CHAPTER 11

Increasing Monthly Surplus

In this chapter you will learn

- *How to reduce costs in a variety of different ways*
- *Options to consider when trying to increase your income*

Our Four-Headed Hydra needs feeding. And the feed is the monthly surplus generated after taking away our fixed and discretionary expenses from our income. But what if we could increase this? What if we can either increase our income or reduce the discretionary expenses? Then we can feed our savings Hydra more and get to our goals faster – that sounds pretty good. Here are a few ideas on how you can do this – I've split them into reducing expenditure and increasing income.

Reducing expenditure

Cut up credit cards & ask your bank to remove your overdraft

Goodbye credit cards, goodbye overdraft. Hello new, responsible you. The extra interest both credit cards and overdrafts incur are simply money down the drain. If you run a £5,000 credit card debt more or less permanently, you are paying almost £1,000 a year – every year – in interest. That's £1,000 that could have been put into one or more of your investment pots. In the cold light of the day, that doesn't sound very sensible does it? More particularly, how do you expect to fulfil that long-term dream when you're wasting money on that scale? And, with the new savings pots and monitoring of your bank account, you should no longer need credit cards or an overdraft. Get rid of them.

Remove old direct debits

This a great habit to get into every six months or so. Go through all the direct debits on your bank account. Are they all still relevant? Do you need them? Many businesses find the online subscription model very profitable, and the reason for that is that people either forget they have signed up to that subscription or never get around to cancelling it. Most people will have at least one or two that won't stand up to the *Do I still need this* test. Do you need all three of Disney+, Netflix and Amazon Prime? Do you have any old gym memberships? I would be ruthless here, because if you cancel something and find that you miss it, you can always re-sign. It doesn't have to be a big decision. We use things for a while, then why they don't become useful anymore we move on. As Marie Kondo, the queen of decluttering, says: "Give thanks and say goodbye."

Want a bonus? When you get to the end of each month, calculate how much you have saved. Then automate it so that amount gets sent to one of your savings pots. You won't even notice the money is going.

Time to change utility supplier?

The supply of gas and electricity in the UK is subject to some interesting practices, which suppliers get away with because of customer inertia. If you don't change your supplier from time to time, you will almost certainly find that your monthly direct debit has increased to the point where you are running credit balances with your supplier. Instead of the usual practice whereby the supplier provides goods to you (in this case, gas and electricity supplies) and then charges you, suppliers are charging in advance. This is good business for them, because you are acting as their bank – the money you have stored with them in the form of credit balances means that they can reduce the amount they borrow from their bankers and therefore cut their interest payments. Good for them, but not so for you. Get online, see what your current balances are, and find a new supplier – ideally, one with a four or five-star rating from the Citizens Advice Bureau. It's painless, because your new supplier will handle the whole of the transfer from the existing one. One of my clients recently cut his expenditure on gas and electricity by nearly £460 a year. That's better in your pocket than the utilities, is it not?

It's not just power companies – think phones, broadband, gyms.

A number of these companies rely on a rather strange business model – they want to keep their customers lazy. This means these companies can either slowly increase prices for the same service, or keep the same cost but not pass on their more competitive rates they give to their new customers. Mobile phone companies are a classic example. Remember when it actually used to cost money to make a phone call? It doesn't anymore, yet a number of people still operate (and more importantly pay for) in that world where they assume they should be paying for calls. And many mobile phone companies rely on this because people's expectations haven't changed. As an example, I recently switched off a phone contract – which had been redundant for about two years – to a new contract that costs me £10 per month. I hadn't previously moved, because I was used to paying £30 per month for a phone and that "felt" like it was the right amount. Once you start looking around you will be amazed at what you find.

The other factor that you can use with these companies is they will throw discounts at you to keep you – again, simply because you're being active and have researched the other options out there. If you call to save you're leaving, you have a very high chance of being offered a much better deal to stay. It's worth a try and it nearly works for any company where you are paying a monthly subscription price.

Do you change your insurance each year?

Have a look at your car, house and contents insurance, because that's another business that exploits long-term customers. An increase of only 2.5% a year soon mounts up to a considerable extra sum of money. And, when you're looking for a new insurer, don't restrict your search to the websites that claim to find you the best deal. They will only recommend an insurer who pays them to do so. Some of the best insurers – Direct Line and the NFU are obvious examples – don't pay those fees and will therefore never be recommended. But the deal they offer may be the best you can get. So find the time to go to their website and ask.

Commute by bike or walk

Cycling or walking to work not only saves significant money, but also provides the added benefit of a lift in both your physical and your mental health. It takes a bit to get organised (and remembering how to change a bike tyre can be challenging) but the overall benefits to your head, heart and wallet are significant. As a proud MAMIL (middle-aged man in Lycra), I can't recommend cycling enough but it may not be for everybody. My business partner proudly walks one hour to work through South-West London every day. And every day he arrives with some idea that he wants to introduce to the business from the podcast he has listened to. Using that time to be productive is fantastic. Your bank account and your mind will thank you for it.

Claim all your tax reliefs

Work from home at all? You can claim tax relief for part of the household bills. Give money to charity? You can claim on that too. Depending on your situation, having an accountant do your tax return may make financial sense. The calculation is fairly easy. Does the accountant find more in tax relief than his/her fees are? If so, great. Then you also have the option of using their calculations and reliefs they find for the following year – if the numbers are still relevant – and submit the return yourself saving the fees. Just don't tell the accountant I told you to do it!

Check your employer benefits

If you work for a large employer, chances are they will have an employee benefits page on the intranet. Many companies are happy to sign up to these and offer staff a discount because they see it as "free" advertising. Great – use it. Log on and take a look at the different offers available. As is always the case with these things not all the discounts will be relevant to you, but sometimes you will find very good deals. Childcare options, healthcare plans, electrical goods tend to be commonly featured. I remember regularly using the "15% off car hire" deal when I was with my old employer.

Ask for a discount

Asking for a discount tends to work on larger purchases where the salesperson has been given some flexibility in the price to make the sale. However it can also work on other purchases that you may not have considered – gym memberships, car hire. Anywhere where there is a person involved can work. You just have to ask, but there are ways of asking that increase your chances. Former FBI negotiator Chris Vos has a great strategy on how to ask for discounts. He calls is using the "Chris method".[19] The theory is you humanise yourself. Most sales people generally have a small amount they are able to discount any price by. Our job as consumers is to use it. As this is a human interaction, it's also amazing (yet when we think about it not surprising), how successful you can be simply being friendly and nice. Nobody wants to deal with an asshole. Everybody is just doing their job and is looking for a good human interaction. Next time you're buying something, go ahead and ask for a discount, but do it with a cheeky smile. Say "My name is <your name>, can I get the <your name> discount?" Watch for the reaction or smile or laugh as that is a good sign that it may work. Give it a try.

---

19 Vos, Chris *Never Split the Difference* p. 180

Finally... Spend freely on your Treat pot

That may sound an odd thing to include in a section on how to spend less, but because you're spending from a finite account each month you won't overspend – and that is the key. Keeping your treat spending allocated to the one account and not slipping money over from the everyday account both makes you think more about your spending, and also keeps a closer track.

Increasing your available income

The above are simple, relatively easy ways to save money each month and you may already have thought of them. But now we get to the interesting bit. It's likely no one has told you this before, but experience of working in large and small organisations has shown me strategies which may not work immediately but, if you try them, will give you a much better chance of increasing your income.

Strategies to earn more

This is the fun bit. This is the part nobody tells you about. Yes, you can switch from a café-bought flat white every day to instant coffee but that tends to be mind-numbingly soul-destroying – trust me, I've done it and I'm happily back on my one flat white per day. Following are a couple of suggestions to help you increase your earnings. They require work, patience and planning – but you aren't expecting anyone to give you money for nothing, now, are you?

Sell old stuff

I was flabbergasted to read the average woman in the U.K accumulates an estimated £22,000 worth of unworn clothes over a lifetime. And its nearly £11,000 for a man.[20] Many resale platforms have popped up over the last few years – it's not just eBay anymore – like Depop and Vinted which specialise in selling (and buying) unwanted clothing.

---

20 https://www.statista.com/statistics/970513/unworn-clothing-british-men-and-women/

Facebook Marketplace is also another site that you can try and sell virtually anything. If you're like me you have enough clutter around the house and so a good clean-up is necessary every six months or so. Items such as old iPhones still attract reasonable prices because the parts are reused or they are sold as reconditioned phones. I bet you would be surprised what you can raise by doing this regularly.

Get promoted

Yes, I know that sounds a bit facile. I also know that it may feel impossible for some people. But it worked for at least one, because I have a client who told me, "I focused on finding the most annoying problem the company I work for had to deal with. And I didn't rest till I'd solved it. It might have earned me nothing, but in fact it got me a promotion. With that promotion came an 8% pay rise and that 8% – all of it – less tax is what I invest." So, at least for one person and probably for more, it's an option.

Another way to think about it is in time. In one of my previous lives as a management consultant, one of my managers would talk about just focusing on an extra 30 mins per day to get promoted. He used those 30 mins to start doing the next job he wanted. He had reached out to his potential next boss, told her what he wanted to do and asked her what she needed working on. Bingo! You can guess who his next boss asked to apply for the role when it became available.

Start a side hustle

The arrival of the internet has changed the global economy forever. The cost of starting and running a business can be very, very low if you have the right idea and now the key part is finding that idea that's right FOR YOU. Find something you can do that other people will be prepared to pay for. There are many resources available for starting a small business so this is only a really small snapshot to get you started.

First step in this is to think about what you enjoy doing that other people will pay for – this diagram could help. The key to solving this problem is generally the more painful the problem for people, the more they are willing to pay to make it go away.

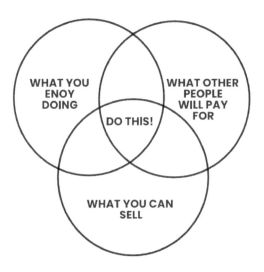

Be creative in your thinking, however one thing many people do when they first start this is to try to create something for everybody. They aim far, far too wide with their potential customer as the thinking goes that the larger the size of the potential customer, the greater the chance of sales. Actually the opposite is true. The more niche your idea is the better, because then it is far easier to define your potential customer. Think of it this way – there are plenty of people making personal training videos and putting them on YouTube, but are there people making videos on how to make the best personal training videos for YouTube? Now your potential customer has moved from a generic "everyone" to a specific "personal trainers who want to post videos on YouTube." See how that way you are solving a specific problem for a specific person.

First step is to think of your niche and define your customer. Then decide what you're going to charge – and don't make the mistake of basing your price on what your product or service costs you to make or deliver. The question that matters is: What's it worth to the person I'm making/doing it for? And that will often be a lot more than your cost.

The final step is to work out how you deliver your product or service to customers. Online is the easiest way to start, by creating a simple website and posting on social media channels – but you will need to supply content consistently to those channels over many days, weeks and months before anything much happens. Given that your chosen niche is something you enjoy doing anyway, this shouldn't be too much of a problem – you are doing something you enjoy.

You may have already thought of this, but don't discount offline ideas as well in terms of helping out with your local community or market. A physical stall or shop has greater set-up costs and requires significantly more investment of your time, but it could be as simple as producing flyers or samples of your work and handing them out at your local train station or wherever your potential customers are. And that's the key point – when you have defined your potential customer, you think about where they hang out, online and in real life.

Whatever you decide to do, creating samples for people to try and/or test is the best way to get started. There is a reason the first thing Gordon Ramsay does in *Kitchen Nightmares* is gets his victims (I mean chefs) to stand outside offering samples to passers-by. People have more confidence buying when they know what they're getting.

This has been only a brief introduction to the idea, but if it is got you excited there are many excellent free resources or books worth reading. My favourite is Tim Ferriss's *4 Hour Work Week*. Give it a look.

CHAPTER 12

Building Knowledge

In this chapter you will learn

- *Why time is the most important factor in growing investments*
- *What risk really means in investing and how to use it to your advantage*

Investment markets are the biggest casinos in the world. I should know as I've spent my whole career working in them. If you don't know what you're doing there are many highly incentivised, sophisticated players who will happily take your money off you. However, just like casinos, with a little knowledge and a basic system in place, you also can do very well from them.

In this chapter I want to explore two of the most important concepts you need to understand about investing – time and risk. I'm going to assume a little bit of prior knowledge in that you know what shares are and how after you buy shares the value goes up and down until you eventually sell for either a profit or loss.

Time

It's very easy to overcomplicate investing. You can tell how easy it is by the number of people who have developed complicated mathematical concepts that claim to be able to value a portfolio precisely and define exactly the portfolio each individual investor should have to meet their needs. If only they worked! And the reason they tend not to work is that they overlook a vital factor in choosing any investment. That factor is time.

You have goals in your life. Your goals are not the same as the goals of the family next door. Nor are they the same as they were ten years ago, and they will have changed again 20 years from now. Your financial plan needs to match your goals. Isn't that why you're reading this book? What's more, the goals that you have for your life two years from now and your 40-year goals are very different.

Now think of this at a higher level in terms of every participant in investment markets. Every individual and/or fund buying and selling shares in an investment market has their particular goals based on time. Some are very high-frequency short-term traders who just want to make a couple of pence or cents on every trade, but they do this millions of times a day. Others are sophisticated hedge funds implementing sophisticated strategies whilst others are more long-term holding pension funds. For every transaction in the markets, there is always a buyer and a seller. Their reasons for being on the different sides of that transaction are their own, but are principally driven by their own time-based goals.

That's the importance of time.

Let's for a moment consider two portfolios. One follows the pattern investment advisers usually call "low risk" meaning that, while the long-term average return is round about 4.5% fluctuations in either direction won't exceed 15% as a typical maximum. The other, which those same advisers would call "higher risk", can fluctuate up to 40% in any given year and in either direction, but the long-term trend will always be positive and the average long-term increase will be around 7%.

What those two portfolios illustrate is an inescapable fact of investing: if you are prepared to accept that fluctuations both up and down can be greater, the long-term return will be higher. It's a sad fact of life (and investing) that, if you want to avoid extreme fluctuations, you must accept a lower long-term return. The consequence of this impacts how we should construct our personal investment strategy. £100,000 invested at an average 4.5% annual return will, after 25 years, have grown to about £300,000. And that isn't bad. But at an average 7% annual return, 25 years would have seen the £100,000 grow to more than £540,000. In other words, the cost – the financial loss to you – of using a short-term strategy to meet long-term goals is £240,000 for each £100,000 you invested. And that is a price not worth paying. But you would not have been wise to use the long-term strategy to meet short-term goals, because the risk of having your stake plunge by 40% at the very time you need to use it is simply not worth running. We discuss this concept more in the following chapters.

Risk

Risk is not necessarily something to be scared of. In investing, risk is really what drives the long-term returns. Our world has many different risks and frankly the better we are at accepting them rather than trying to artificially control them, the better results we tend to get.

There is the famous story of Long-Term Capital Management (LTCM), a firm that nearly blew up the financial system. This was a firm filled with Nobel Prize winning economists and at least two men who literally designed the calculation on how to value options in investment markets – Fischer Black and Myron Scholes. Unfortunately, this was a case where they were so smart they thought they could control risk for their profit. When the Russian bond market collapsed in 1998 it triggered a series of events that, mathematically in their eyes, could not happen. But they happened and brought down LTCM requiring a bail out from the US Federal Reserve. Appropriately, the key book describing the rise and fall of LTCM is called *When Genius Failed*.

Investment markets have a history of rise and fall, but given long enough, they always tend to rise.

There is an expression common among investment professionals: "Markets climb a wall of worry." There's always something to worry about – and it seems that we always choose the wrong thing.

In 1987, Black Monday saw the collapse of every major stock exchange across the world. This had happened before. Is there no way to know when it will happen again? Unfortunately, there isn't. What experience teaches us is how to deal with a catastrophe like the last one. And the only thing I can promise you about the next catastrophe is that it won't be anything like any we've already had. We haven't a clue what will cause the next market crash. All experience teaches us is that there will be one.

Since Black Monday, there have been four more international disasters:

2000 – Dot-com bust
2001 – 9/11 Twin Towers
2008 – Lehman Brothers bankruptcy
2020 – Covid

Do you know anyone who forecast them? Neither do I. Oh, sure, there were reasons behind the dot-com bust that should and did make some people think (and say), "It can't go on like this. This is a bubble, it's out of control and it will burst." But America's allies, the Saudis, organising jihadists to fly into the World Trade Center? The global financial system nearly imploding because a few Americans didn't pay off their mortgage and nobody knew how much the risk was spread around? And as for the virus – it's not inconceivable that some scientists in China could have told us what was coming, but chose not to in order not to be disappeared by their own government, but there was no way for any Western investor to foresee it. And while it hammered businesses and stock indices when it struck, to slightly misquote Stephen Sondheim, we've been through all this and we're still here.

Before the virus struck, investors worried about all sorts of things. As it turned out, the things they were worrying about really didn't matter. It was something they had never thought of that was about to devastate the market. And that, I submit, is always the case. Yes, investors need to be aware of what is going on – but worrying is pointless because it's almost invariably worry about the wrong thing.

Having these concerns around tends to keep investors less than fully invested. This means there is more potential cash to put to work as these worries gradually disappear, which is the reason for the phrase "markets climb a wall of worry." There will be a crash again at some point in the future, we all know that, but we will never know what the cause is until it's too late.

Nor does it always take something catastrophic like 9/11 or Covid-19. Markets rise and markets crash – that's just what they do. They have always done it and will always do it because markets are simply extensions of our own human emotions – specifically fear and greed.

There are a number of technical factors that push markets around such as liquidity and positioning which I could bore you with for hours, but the simple fact is this: markets keep going up until they don't. Then they drop. And they normally drop much faster than they go up. Once the drop has finished, they start going up again. And repeat. There is always a reason and there is never a reason. Humans sometimes try to provide too many answers and find it difficult just to accept the present state as it is. The quicker you can come round to this, the more successful investor I promise you will be over the long-term.

So we shouldn't worry? I didn't say that. But what is more important is to have in place a financial plan to protect and prepare you for whatever happens. And that plan should take account of risk in its general form.

Risk is there to be managed. But risk management is an expression that raises strange ideas. There are, or appear to be, those who think that, if you're practising risk management, then nothing bad will happen. I'm afraid that isn't true. Bad things will still happen. A financial plan and investment portfolio that takes account of risk management means that no amount of bad things will destroy you financially. It's not about eliminating risk, but both diversifying and even embracing it.

A final word on risk

I'll say it again: Markets go up and markets go down. We start at a point of certainty today because today we know the current price of a stock or index. From here the future is uncertain. This is a key message I need you to understand. The path of the investment is uncertain and volatile and the only way we can have any confidence is by looking at what has happened in the past. I will touch on this in a future chapter but understanding that there will be uncertainty in the future is crucial for you.

Understanding this is not the same as acting on that understanding. Imagine a scenario where at one point you check your investment account and it is down 40% from where it was. How do you react? Do you feel physically sick, panic and withdraw all your funds to make the pain go away? If so, you're entirely normal as that is a natural human emotion when we are faced with severe discomfort. Unfortunately, from a personal finance point of view it is also the single WORST decision you could ever make. Investing is not a sport designed for normal humans as you have to ignore 5,000 or more years of evolutionary biology to become good at it.

Buy low and sell high. It sounds so easy and so obvious, doesn't it? But to do so we're fighting ourselves.

As cavemen our brains were trained to go with the pack, not standing out for fear of being frozen or eaten by a sabre-tooth tiger. Think of this from an investment point of view. The market is going up so you want to buy in and experience the good times you perceive everybody else is enjoying. So your instinct is to buy when the market is high.

Think of the opposite scenario, markets have fallen hard and fast, news reports around the world are about stock market crashes with pictures of men on stock exchange floors running their fingers through their hair. We all know those images. Our natural human reaction to fear is either to run away to make it stop or be frozen solid and unable to think. You want to sell now for fear of running out of money altogether. So your instinct is to sell when the market is low.

Hang on you say, that's not what I'm going to do. I'm different. I'll be able to handle the pressure. Well, I'm sorry but this isn't about you – it's biology.

But there is a way to beat it, and the simple answer is not to play the game. Don't get sucked into trading, being thrown around by market sentiment. Have a plan and stick to it.

How time and risk affect investment planning

Many financial planners, because they want to surround something that is actually fairly simple with an air of mystery (fees have to be justified, right?), prefer to keep secret something that is actually blindingly obvious: in the long term, history shows us that, in stock markets in developed countries like the USA and the UK, markets will always go up. We have 150 years of data to support this. There have been stock market crashes that, at the time, made people think Armageddon was here – but, with time, the value always returned and always exceeded what had been lost. There's a simple reason for that: stock markets are fuelled by money and money has to go somewhere. And that is what we all need to remember. If you have enough years ahead of you and can afford to wait, money invested in the stock market will always show a positive return that exceeds inflation. Stock markets can be highly volatile in the short-term, which is why the money you are likely to need (or even may possibly need) in the short term should not be invested there. But in the long term, the trend is always and will continue to be up. In the 100 years to 2020, the average annual return from the FTSE100 is +7%[21] and the S&P 500 is 10.5%[22] But what about inflation I hear you say. Surely most of those returns are actually just inflation? Well, no. Even after adjusting for inflation, the S&P 500 still averaged 7.4% over the last 100 years[23]

---

21 https://stockmarketalmanac.co.uk/2016/12/100-years-of-the-ftse-all-share-index-since-1917/

22 https://www.officialdata.org/us/stocks/s-p-500/1922?amount=100&endYear=2022

23 ibid

Most people only think of stock markets and investing when there is a crash and it makes the 10 pm news, so they associate it with losing money. This couldn't be further from the truth. The bad news is that most people will probably never learn this lesson. The good news is you just have!

To summarise, time and risk are both your friends for medium (and long) term investing. It is just a case of holding your nerve through the inevitable stock market crashes. It may be simple, but it's not easy. At the point of maximum stress, please try to come back to this part of the book. It may well save you thousands of pounds in terms of the actions you chose NOT to take. Don't be scared out of markets. You have a cash safety net in place to help you with this precise time. So you don't need to sell. You just hold your nerve and trust in history. Markets always work in cycles and there will always be a new cycle coming. You just need to wait.

CHAPTER 13

Constructing the Investment Strategy

In this chapter you will learn

- *How to build your own personalised investment strategy*
- *How to think in terms of short, medium and long-term timeframes*
- *How to think about investment risk and where you fit in on the spectrum of risk*
- *What are the best types of investments to use?*

Before creating any investment plan, we need to utilise the two biggest factors in investing that we discussed in the last chapter – time and risk – and then make them work specifically for you.

Short, Medium & Long

The easiest way to do this is to start thinking about planning your investment strategy to match your goals. You need one set of investments – one portfolio – for your immediate goals, one for your medium-term goals and one for your retirement goals. The immediate portfolio is almost certainly very low on risk, because it is concerned among other things with covering emergency needs. It will probably contain only cash and near-cash equivalents. The retirement portfolio will be very different because, if it bobs up and down in the short term, and even if the downs are quite big, the long-term trend will be up (the long-term trend is always up) and that's the only thing that matters.

Most people invest for one reason only to make their money work harder so there is more than what they put in when they go to use it. Investing is one of the few places where one plus one can really equal three. The key determining factor of actually how to invest is to think in terms of the timing of when you will actually need the money.

You can think of it like a ladder.

IMMEDIATE	SHORT	MEDIUM	LONG
1–2 YRS	3–5 YRS	6–10 YRS	11+ YRS

I tend to split the times up as follows:

Immediate needs where you will need the funds in the first 1–2 years.

Short-term needs where you will want to access the funds over the next 3–5 years

Medium-term needs where you will want to access the funds over the next 6–10 years

And Long-term needs are at 11+ years.

Let's begin with immediate needs. This is where you will want to use these funds over the next 1–2 years. There is a very simple answer to how you should invest this money and it's one word: cash.

Want to put money away for two years or under – cash.

This is very simple, because there's only one safe haven for your short-term money, and that haven is cash. You're going to keep everything you save for your immediate needs in cash. Why? It's a matter of risk. To put it at its simplest, you simply can't risk seeing the value of your funds that you will need within two years crash just when you need it. Suppose, for example, one of your short-term objectives was to have enough to put a deposit on a new home in two years' time. The two years are almost up, your deposit will be due in a week's time, and everything looks good because you had that money invested in the markets and it has been growing nicely for almost two years, exactly as you hoped it would do. And then – exactly as markets tend to do sometimes – it drops by 20%. Over time, that money and more will come back in due course but your deposit isn't due in due course. It's due next week.

Clearly, that is not a risk you can take. And the only way to avoid it is to keep the immediate-term funds in cash form. Over the long term, money held in the right investments will always increase because it follows the market and over the long term the market will always rise. More on this later. It doesn't know any other way to perform. But over the short-term, it can go down as well as up and Murphy's Law says it will go down at just the moment that will cause you maximum damage. And if you feel like ignoring Murphy's Law, bear in mind the rider to that law which says: Murphy was an optimist.

When thinking about other options you can't invest in property on a short-term basis and everything else – gold, crypto, currencies even bonds are too volatile to serve a purpose.

To my mind, cash is potential energy in the pure physics definition. Cash in itself is nothing; what makes it matter is the opportunity to use it do something useful – to buy a new boiler, upgrade a flight or even buy a house. With interest and savings rates where they currently are, cash by itself sitting in a savings account, does nothing. However, what it CAN do is the most important part and that is why having an amount of cash stashed away is vitally important. Cash is potential. Cash is flexibility. Cash is the option to make your own decisions at your timing and not somebody else's.

Sounds great I know, but this can go too far. Why is cash more dangerous longer-term?

Leaving cash in an account for a long period of time is not only pointless, it is destructive. Compound interest is what makes value rise. It also works in the opposite direction.

Imagine you have cash sitting in a standard savings account and you are getting 0.5% interest. Now, typically inflation runs along at ~2.5% per year, but it's amazing how much higher than that it goes for all the important and/or fun things. Think about school fees or concert tickets or Sky subscriptions. They all definitely go up by more than 2.5% per year, but for the sake of this exercise let's generalise to say everything goes up by 2.5% per year.

So, in reality you are LOSING 2% per year in value on your cash – the cost of everything is going up by 2.5% yet you're only receiving 0.5%. If you do nothing with your cash, after five years you have lost over 10%. After ten years you are down nearly 22% in real value of that cash.

Therefore cash can also be lazy and destructive to your real wealth.

What I'm asking you to do is to think about the cash you hold in relation to the cash you need. Earlier on in the book I asked you to define how much cash you think you need on hand for opportunities or a safety net. The key point is that that's the amount you should hold in cash and that's ALL you should hold in cash. It doesn't matter if you're losing a real value of 2% per year if the cash is sitting there for a specific reason.

Build that cash pot (or Rainy Day fund) and leave it there. If any opportunities come or go, then you can adjust that cash amount that you have in savings. See, you've come a long way from that piggy bank.

Short-term (3–5 years) and Medium-term (6–10 years)

It's over this period where we need to get a little more personal in terms of thinking how you feel about risk.

I described risk in detail in the last chapter but to get a little more practical here I'll describe how we, as financial planners, look at your risk level and how it determines your investment strategy.

Typically most financial planners will ask their clients, or prospective clients, to complete a risk questionnaire and the way you answer the questionnaire will typically put you on a spectrum that looks like this:

Range 1 to 5
1 – No risk
2 – Cautious
3 – Balanced
4 – Growth
5 – Adventurous.

Many planners will have different names for the categories, and sometimes the scores are out of 10, some out of 7, but essentially they are all very similar.

You can see a sample of an attitude to risk questionnaire at the website www.adamwalkom.com

The key determining factor for all of these sectors is how much volatility (a fancy word describing ups and downs) can you as an investor handle. And remembering our risk discussion from last chapter, the greater volatility you can handle, the higher the long-term growth rate you should expect.

A useful short-cut is to think about the volatility in terms of potential returns per year. This chart below should help.

Hypothetical returns per risk category in any one year.

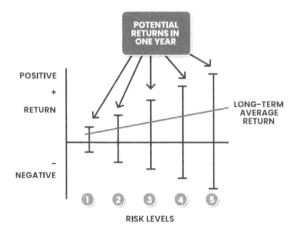

As you move up the risk categories, you can see the average return increasing, however you can also see the size of the potential returns also decreasing.

Another key factor to think about is how much will you freak out when you see your money go down. Some people can easily brush this off as they understand that ups and downs are all part of long-term investing. Others have an almost visceral reaction to loss and it causes a huge amount of stress. There is no correct answer and everybody is different. A rule of thumb for this factor is the more comfortable you are with loss (and volatility) the higher risk category you can look to take on.

How to apply this:

So for the short and medium-term needs we have a bit of flex in terms of your investment plan which will be determined by how comfortable you are with taking risk. Based on the principle around time again, you should keep the short-term category one risk level below the medium-term category. Remember you will need the short-term funds sooner, so you don't want the big volatility coming into when you access the funds.

So, for a "Cautious investor", their risk levels may look like this:

TIME	IMMEDIATE 1-2 YRS	SHORT 3-5 YRS	MEDIUM 6-10 YRS	LONG 11+ YRS
RISK LEVEL	CASH	CASH	CAUTIOUS	BALANCED

And for a "Balanced investor", it could look like this:

TIME	IMMEDIATE 1-2 YRS	SHORT 3-5 YRS	MEDIUM 6-10 YRS	LONG 11+ YRS
RISK LEVEL	CASH	CAUTIOUS	BALANCED	ADVENTUROUS

And finally for an "Adventurous investor", it could look like this:

TIME	IMMEDIATE 1-2 YRS	SHORT 3-5 YRS	MEDIUM 6-10 YRS	LONG 11+ YRS
RISK LEVEL	CASH	BALANCED	ADVENTUROUS	ADVENTUROUS

To try and make it relative, I set up my own personal portfolio along the lines of the adventurous investor. Why this way for me? Keep reading and I'll explain.

Long-term investing

The only way to build real wealth is own equity – that can be either owning 100% of your own business or 0.0001% of Amazon – either works. This way you are owning all or part of a productive asset that is producing and growing value for you over time. If you think about equity in a property, this also can apply. I will talk about property in another section, but for this section I'm focusing on equity, and the specific form of equity being shares in companies.

Think about the main asset classes you potentially can invest in – stocks (or equities), bonds, property and what are called alternative assets (like currencies, commodities, private equity, bitcoin, art, wine, etc., etc.). It's a long list, but the main asset classes are stocks, bonds and property. Cash is not an asset class, because you don't 'invest' in cash. You simply hold it to use at some other time as we discussed previously.

The chart below gives you some context in terms of long-term returns. Stocks are the winners by a mile.

Long-Term Returns for Equities Are Higher Than for Other Asset Classes

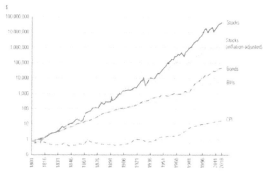

Source: Valuation: Measuring and Managing the Value of Companies, University Edition, 7th Edition

Bear in mind the outperformance of equities is so large over the 200-year period of this chart, the scale they have used is logarithmic.

So why do equities do so much better? Because you are investing in real businesses, in real people growing businesses over time and increasing profits. Because these businesses get to exploit all the capital growing capabilities of inflation, technology and human ingenuity for the benefit of their shareholders (and, most of the time, their other stakeholders and that includes their customers). Equities are the only asset class that allows you, as an individual, to take advantage of this leverage anywhere in the world. Owning equities allows you to increase your personal wealth.

Bonds, on the other hand, are simply loans. You lend your money either to the government or to a company; in return, they promise to pay you interest at a fixed rate for the life of the bond then to pay you back the full sum at the end. The market value of bonds is determined by current interest rates and how they compare to the bond's interest rate. A bond which promises to pay 5% per year when other interest rates are around 2% should trade for a higher figure than ("at a premium to") the original sum invested, and vice versa.

The key difference between bonds and equities is that the bond is just debt – you don't get to participate in the upside.

You get no benefit from the company or government doing well; all you get is your money back. If the company or government does badly the only advantage is that your money may be paid back before equity holders receive anything, but this happens very rarely and only normally in dire economic situations.

Bonds in theory offer lower volatility, however the experience of 2022 taught us that that is not always the case. Your only perspective for your retirement pot should be long-term wealth building and bonds won't give you that.

In terms of property, this is an area that tends to divide people. Some people love property investing because they can see it – it's "bricks and mortar" and probably a lot less confusing than pensions and financial markets. However there are a number of reasons I steer clear of it, from a long-term investment point of view. Just a caveat here, when I'm talking about investing in property, I am talking about buying a second property, or buy-to-let or investment property and not about owning a home. Owning a home is a part financial and part emotional decision. You have to live somewhere and you may as well own it as property values tend go up over time. The emotional value comes with the fact that this is your home – a lot of the major milestones in your life happen at this home and there will be many memories attached to the home. There is value in this. Also from a pure financial aspect, by owning your own home either outright or through a mortgage, you will have a serious amount of your wealth already tied up in the property sector. Owning just your own home is relatively tax-effective as well. Yes, you need pay stamp duty to purchase a property, however there is no capital gains tax (CGT) on sale of your main residence. That is not the case on investment properties. In fact, the CGT for higher rate taxpayers is higher on property at 28% versus investments at 20%. You also cannot claim all your mortgage expenses if you're a higher rate taxpayer.[24] From a long-term investment perspective, it is best just to stick to equities.

---

24 Tax rules correct at time of writing October 2022.

But what type of equities and how do I invest in them?

For my pension and other long-term investments, I use 100% equity index funds (also known as tracker funds). An index fund is a fund that invests in a way that is virtually identical to the major stock indices around the world – the FTSE 100 in the UK, the S&P500 in the US, the Eurostox50 in Europe or the Nikkei225 in Japan. An index fund does the work for you. It spreads your investment across multiple different companies and you get the market performance of that index. They are simple, cheap and very effective. However, they have flown under the radar for many years because they are not as profitable for the fund management industry. You will I'm sure have seen the advertisements for the fund management industry with their huge marketing budgets who all will tell you they can beat the market. I'll let you in on a secret, most of them cannot. Around 82% of managed funds failed to beat the market over a 20-year period[25] and, bad as that may sound, the reality is worse because not included in those figures are the funds that did so badly that they didn't survive 20 years.

A managed fund differs from a tracker fund in that managed fund managers are basing decisions on their own analysis of the companies whose shares they are buying and selling. Index funds, on the other hand, simply follow the market. There will always be certain managed funds that outperform the market for a short-period of time, but the point is a) you can never pick when that time will be and b) it will work for a while, then it will stop working as the underlying market and economic situation changes.

The other advantage around tracking the index, is that the index itself will do the rebalancing for you. The major stock indices around the world all will reflect the best companies in their regions, so as companies grow and get to a certain size, they will be added to the index. The indices tend to have only a fixed number of companies (the clue is in the name, the FTSE

---

25 *Index Trackers vs Managed Funds*, The Motley Fool UK, 2020

100, the S&P500, the Nikkei225) so adding a growing company will be at the expense of another company whose fortunes have fallen and is taken out of the index. Thereby you get this natural rebalancing towards the largest, fastest growing, most successful companies and away from those companies that are underperforming. Magic.

And the final, potentially single most important advantage index funds have over managed funds? They are cheaper. One golden rule of finance: You can never be sure about future performance but you can always be sure about today's costs. Investing in a low-cost strategy is one of the key investment decisions you can make. Let's look at an example: If you invest £50,000 in a fund that costs you 0.09% per year, versus one that costs you 0.49% per year – which is a typical managed fund charge. Assuming an average growth rate of 6%, you will be £11,491 better off after 20 years and amazingly £30,042 better off after 30 years.[26]

That's why low-cost index funds are the best option.

---

26 https://investor.vanguard.com/investment-products/mutual-funds/low-cost#modal-chart-desc

CHAPTER 14

Putting the Investment Strategy into Practice – Part 1

In this chapter you will learn

- *Why flexibility is so important in your financial planning*
- *What investment accounts to use for your strategy, and in what order of priority*
- *About the type of funds I normally recommend to my clients, and why*
- *How the plan comes together and thinking about future contributions*

In the previous chapter we looked at what amount you were going to keep in cash as well establishing appropriate risk levels for your short and medium-term investments. We also discussed the benefits of 100% equity index funds for long-term investments, but I hear you asking "That's great in theory Adam, but how does it impact me and my situation?" In this chapter, I'm going to show you.

As we've mapped out the theoretical plan which looks great in paper, now we will put it into practice in terms of some of the current savings, investments or pensions that you currently own.

The value of flexibility and of having real options

I have already mentioned the importance of flexibility in your financial plan, but now I want to expand on that discussion and bring in the idea of creating real options for yourself. You don't hear much from the investment industry about time and flexibility because they have not found a way to turn them into products. If they can't make products, they have nothing to sell, and if they have nothing to sell, then funnily enough they tend not to talk about them. But this is where you, as an individual investor, have an advantage. You can make the decisions that are best for you based on all the different factors that we discuss in this book. With a little knowledge and perhaps help from me, you are unstoppable and all the financial dreams we've discussed are yours for the taking. But you do need a bit of flexibility in your plans. We all know – or we do if we give it a moment's thought – that life is not linear. In his book *Antifragile*, Nassim Taleb talks a lot about volatility and how the more intelligent someone is, the more likely they are to fall into the trap of thinking that volatility in everything can be removed or "managed away". The usual reason for believing this is that they have studied or committed to a theory (usually promoted by highly paid management consultants) which they apply to real-world situations. The further down the path people take this, the more trouble they tend to find themselves in when the inevitable happens and a totally unexpected event blows the theory out of the water taking the business/people/idea with it.

Harold Macmillan, former UK prime minister, when asked what had blown his government off course, famously replied, "Events, dear boy. Events." It's the same for all of us. We don't know what the events will be, but we know they're going to happen.

So how can we prepare for the unexpected, when we have no idea what it will be? By building flexibility into our plans. By not stretching or overextending ourselves in any particular direction and keeping that buffer of cash secure and handy. By giving ourselves real options.

And this is not just talking about the boiler blowing up or needing to travel internationally at very short notice. This is giving yourself the option to buy a bigger house in a few years' time because you've been disciplined about paying down the mortgage. This is not overcommitting into your pension scheme or children's Junior ISAs, because that money is not accessible if you ever need it. This is deciding to stop work early because you want to spend more time with family or start a passion project at age 55 because you have the money in the bank and have done the forecasting to ensure that you will never run out of money in your lifetime. All of these are real options and all are available to you, depending on what you decide, because you built flexibility into your plans.

The best example of looking at the misunderstood value of having real options was provided by Michael Maboussin, an acclaimed research analyst and author when he was at Credit Suisse First Boston back in 1999. Maboussin wrote an investment report on real options and highlighted a number of companies who were very good at it. There was, however, one company he highlighted as standing out way above the rest in 1999. Let's see if you can guess it through his description:

"Nowhere does a real options approach apply more than at a company like X. In fact, options thinking is built into the culture, which stresses flexibility and adaptation"

Can you guess what company is X? He was talking about Amazon. At the point of publication of that report on June 23rd 1999, Amazon's share price closed at $58.90. As I write this today its $3,165.[27] That's a significant rise in value for understanding and using real options.

Having flexibility and options built into your own planning can, like Amazon, also create enormous value for you in your own life.

Building your plan with flexibility

First take stock of what you have. Split it into cash (savings, premium bonds, cash ISAs etc), investments (investment ISAs, shares) and pensions.

We will start by looking at Cash:

---

27 Maboussin, Michael *Get Real – Using Real Options in Security Analysis*

Cash.

By putting in place the savings plan I mentioned in the previous chapter you should have built your safety net here. The total value of this pot should be safety net plus any other major expenses you have upcoming over the next 2 years.

Example could be: £20,000 safety net plus kitchen/bathroom renovation of £20,000 = total £40,000 in cash.

For the above example if you have more than £40,000 in savings at the moment, then that is great, great news. We then can move some of the cash over to the investment. If you don't have that level of cash, you have two ways to solve it. Either ramp up the savings plan as described in the previous chapter, or sell-down some of your investments and move them into safer cash. By selling down investments, clearly they will lose the option for growth, but more importantly they won't go down and that is the key to ensuring the money is there for those expenses in the next couple of years. If I had to choose between the two, then clearly the savings plan is the better option as we want to try to avoid taking money out of investments as much as possible.

How to hold the cash?

The simplest way is to find an easy-access direct saver account that pays a small amount of interest. This cash is not meant to be there for earning money so don't worry too much about the rate. Also trying to be clever on interest rates (remember the disaster of the Icelandic banks?) can cause trouble. One of the best accounts to hold cash in is the NS&I Direct Saver account. As NS&I is an offshoot of HM Treasury it is not technically a bank. Therefore it is not backed by the current £85,000 Financial Services Compensation Scheme (FSCS) that all bank accounts are covered. Isn't that bad? No, it has better coverage. It's backed by the U.K. Government and as the U.K can print its own banknotes, technically it can never go bankrupt. This is the only account available to individuals that is 100% guaranteed. So use it.

So we've established our cash pot.

Investments

First step is to review everything you have. Where is it? How much is it worth? What type of account is it held in – ISA or General Investment Account (GIA) or investment bond?

The best accounts to hold investments

Maximise ISAs.

Everyone should know about individual savings accounts (ISAs). ISAs are brilliant. Put simply, everything that goes into an ISA is tax-free forever – income, growth, dividends etc. None of these get taxed if the money is in an ISA. You also can put up to £20,000 per year[28] per person and this restarts every tax year (so April). Cash ISAs are basically pointless but for one good reason. You can transfer them across into investment ISAs (which are also annoyingly called "stocks and shares ISAs"). In fact, all ISAs can be transferred without losing their tax-free status and this is generally a good idea to consolidate.

Step 1 – Find your preferred investment platform which has an ISA on it.

Step 2 – Consolidate ISAs onto this platform (including Cash ISAs if they are left over from you cash safety net above)

Step 3 – Consider selling down whatever shares you own (up to a value £20,000) to use your ISA allowance for this tax year. Careful with this step as if they shares are held in a GIA or other taxable account, you may need to pay CGT on the shares. However, as you are selling a total of £20,000, the shares would have had to have done very well to generate a profit above the annual CGT allowance of £12,300.[29]

Step 4 – Transfer the rest of your investments onto the same platform using "in-specie" transfers. An in-specie transfer is where you don't actually sell the investments, you just re-register them to the new platform. The platform can help you with this. Transferring this way means you don't face any tax implications

---

28 Correct as of tax year 2022–23
29 Correct as of tax year 2022–23

and consolidates all your investments onto the one platform for ease of use.

Now that you have all your investments on one platform, go back to the previous chapter and look at your attitude to risk score.

Think about what sort of funds you will need for the short, medium and long-term holding periods. We've already done this work back in the earlier chapters of the book. See how it's all connected?

As an example, if you have say £60,000 total in investments here, you can split them into 3 x £20,000 blocks for short, medium and long term.

Using the risk ladder we've built, you can find low-cost funds which help you invest using the rough asset allocation model from before. For example here, I have assumed a Balanced investor which has an risk level per timeline as below:

TIME	IMMEDIATE 1–2 YRS	SHORT 3–5 YRS	MEDIUM 6–10 YRS	LONG 11+ YRS
RISK LEVEL	CASH	CAUTIOUS	BALANCED	ADVENTUROUS

An example of some of the funds you could use are:

Vanguard Lifestrategy range

Blackrock MyMap range

Legal & General Multi-index range

HSBC Global Strategy Range.

Each of the large fund providers has a range of funds suitable for your risk preference levels and each of those ranges mentioned above are relatively low-cost.

Key tip for choosing funds: Make sure you choose funds which have the acronym "Acc" after it and NOT (Inc). Acc stands for accumulation which means any dividends or interest will be reinvested for you in the fund giving your further growth. If you choose

Inc., this means Income and the dividends and interest will be paid out into a cash account attached to your fund. Most people then forget about and/or don't need that cash and it deducts from overall performance. So remember, choose the Acc version of the fund.

When choosing the funds, it doesn't necessarily matter which funds are in the ISA and which are in a GIA. The entire pot is what counts in terms of splitting out for short, medium and long as you can have different funds in either the ISA or GIA.

An example of what I'm talking about could look like this

Platform – Hargeaves Lansdown

£45,000 in ISA, £15,000 in GIA.

Person is a Balanced investor.

Within ISA

£20,000 Vanguard Lifestragey 100% Equity – Long-term investment

£20,000 Vanguard Lifestrategy 60% Equity – Medium-term investment

£5,000 Vanguard Lifestrategy 40% Equity – Short-term investment.

Within GIA

£15,000 Vanguard Lifestratey 40% Equity – Short-term investment.

Note how the higher-growth, longer-term options are in the ISA because of its tax-free growth status.

Allocating money in the future

There you go – the cash and the investment parts of the plan are set-up – and like all good plans, they generally go out of date on day 1 because of the simple fact that things change – markets, governments, your life, objectives, costs, needs etc., etc. It all continues to change.

However, the whole point of this plan is the inbuilt flexibility it has within it to deal with the constant changes required.

For example, say you decide you want to move house in the next few years and figure you will need to use all the funds for the deposit? No problem. Simply change the fund structure from short-medium-long all down to short. In the case above, this would mean switching all funds into Vanguard Lifestrategy 40% equity. See how easy that is?

Then as your savings continue to build up, you can put more money into these strategies. Do this using the bucket strategy. Just like you were filling up four buckets, use your funds coming in like the water. Fill the first bucket (cash) up first, and once that is full, then move to the short-term bucket. Once that is full, then move to medium term and so on.

Cash -> Short -> Medium -> Long

Hopefully this means as you continue to this, eventually you will just be saving into the long-term bucket as all your other buckets become full up. This is what you want to aim for.

Rebalancing

As time moves on, remember that each of your goals for the short and medium time horizon will become reality. The best way to make sure the plan and structure is the correct one is to do a simple annual review. By conducting an annual review of this structure, you can confirm if the specific time-related goals are still appropriate then make any adjustments to the funds that are deemed necessary.

For the parents out there, an example is those school or university fees for the children that felt a long-way off when you started the plan are all of a sudden looming on the horizon. The fund choice needs to be adjusted to reflect this each year.

Also, if you are making direct debit contributions into your investments you can also use these annual reviews to ensure these still feel like the correct amounts.

Another good exercise for the annual review is a quick direct debit audit like we discussed in the savings section.

CHAPTER 15

Putting the Investment Strategy into Practice – Part 2

In this chapter you will learn

- *Why pensions are so important*
- *How to conduct a DIY pension review*
- *Why pensions are virtually always long-term investments*
- *To spot a dangerous default that has crept into pensions recently*

After building out the first part of the investment strategy in the previous chapter, we finally get to possibly the most misunderstood investment vehicle out there. Pensions.

Pensions are so important they deserve to have an entire chapter dedicated to them. Why?

Your pension is the second largest asset you are ever likely to own… and most people ignore it. Think about that for a second. Think about the amount of time people put into researching phones, cars, clothes, shoes, whatever. Any of those purchases will have virtually no impact on your long-term financial health and happiness. But your pension will.

Imagine this scenario. A long-lost aunt dies and leaves you a house. It's not worth as much as your current house, but it's a nice enough house in a nice location and totally mortgage free. And the only restriction with the house is that you need to keep it until you're 55 (if you're currently younger than that), otherwise then you're free to do whatever you like with it.

So what do you do? Well if you're like most people, you start by feeling slightly guilty that you never really made much effort with that aunt. But very quickly you get over that and think about what's the best thing to do with the house. Does it need any work? How can you tidy it up? What's the best way to maximise the potential growth and/or income (i.e. rent) from the house. The most important thing is you actually think about it.

Why don't people do that with their pensions?

Well some do, but when its eventually too late. The typical response to getting your annual pension statement is to try to read it, have no comprehension of what you're looking at, so ignore it and file it away in the bottom drawer. Does that sound familiar? Twelve months go by and you repeat the exact same process. Let me remind you, this piece of paper that is being ignored is your financial livelihood from age 55 onwards. It's your bread and butter, gas bills, holidays and petrol. And you're just throwing it in the bottom drawer without a second thought.

I want to start a pension crusade. I want people to start thinking about their pensions before it's too late. Do you know what charges you're paying? Do you know how your funds have performed? Do you even know where they are? Well, I'm sorry to say, but you should. It deserves better. You deserve better.

How to conduct your own pension review

The best way to find out more about your pensions is first of all, actually find them. You would be amazed how many people I speak to admit they have lost pensions dotted around somewhere that they cannot remember. So first step, is to find them. Look back through old payslips, old files. Changing the address on an old pension is the last thing many people think about when moving home, so it is that type of pension that easily becomes forgotten.

Once you've located the pensions now take a look at each of them. They generally will be split into two types of pensions

– defined contribution (DC) or defined benefit (DB). The easiest way to tell the difference is that DC pensions will generally have a total value and will also tell you what fund the pension is invested in. DC pensions are normally relatively straightforwards but some can have a few quirks. A DB pension on the other hand is not actually a pot of money that is invested. It is a promise from the pension scheme (Civil Service, Local Government. Teacher's Pension and NHS are some of the more common ones) to pay you a certain amount per year GUARANTEED from a certain date. It is this guarantee part that is vital. DB pensions have become much rarer over the years as put simply, they have become too costly for most employers to run. But this is why they are so valuable from an employee or member perspective. A good rule of thumb is if you have a DB pension, don't touch it. You don't normally need to do anything to maintain it – apart from keep your address updated – as the amount promised normally goes up with inflation each year. Just before the nominated pay out date arrives, they will get in touch and ask where you want to be paid – bingo. So, if you are lucky enough to have one of these DB schemes, put these aside and just make sure your details are all correct.

If on the other hand you have either one or more DC pensions, then these require a little more work to review them.

DC Pension review

Step 1 – Calculate total amounts. You would be amazed how many people do not include pensions when they are thinking about their total wealth.

Step 2 – Look at each pension and find out what fund or funds it is invested in. From each pension provider then download a factsheet of that particular fund and look for the asset allocation (what percentage shares vs bonds vs property vs cash etc), fund performance and fund charges.

Step 3 – Try to find if there are any hidden guarantees, bonuses or conversely exit charges or penalties within each pension. A neat trick is to look for a transfer value. Does the transfer value equal the fund value? Then there is unlikely any of these and you are fine. If the transfer value is different to the fund value, then there is something going on that needs to be investigated further. Also, if your pension started before 2006, then look for something called an A-day value. I won't detail what this is, but it means there may be extra tax-free cash available for that particular pension than is larger than the standard 25%. Ask the provider these questions and they will tell you.

Step 4 – For any DC pension that has no guarantees, bonuses or anything that potentially changes the value, look to consolidate these. For the others, again best to leave for now.

Step 5 – Best place for consolidating pensions is either your current employer pension or the investment platform where all your other investments sit (ISA/GIA etc.).

Rule of thumb (1) – If your employer pension is with NEST, Peoples Pension, NOW pensions, all of these are very basic auto-enrolment scheme that are very limited in their offering. Some only have one fund available. These are not the best options to consolidate into.

Rule of thumb (2) – Your current employer pension should give you discounts on the costs of your pension. Firms like Legal & General are very competitive on their pricing. Find out the cost of your employer pension and compare it to the platform cost. Use a benchmark of 0.25%. Anything below that is cheap. Anything above that can potentially be done cheaper.

Step 6 – Request transfers of your DC pensions that we discussed in Step 4. To organise this contact either the platform to where you are transferring or your employer pension scheme. It is in their interest for the administrators to make it as easy as possible to transfer in pensions so they are normally helpful.

Step 7 – Think about fund investment.

Let's go back to our short-medium-long term investment structure. Pensions are the ultimate long-term investment as a) you cannot touch them before you are 55 and b) when you do actually retire, they potentially should be accessed last because they have other benefits such as not being included in your estate on your death. How best to draw down your retirement income was covered back in Chapter 8.

And remember how we invest for the long-term?

Low-cost index tracker funds that are 100% equity.

Take a look at the fund offering for ALL your pensions – that is the ones you are leaving behind, your current employer scheme and, if you're using one, the new platform that will potentially receive your pensions. All the pensions should have some sort of low-cost index fund offering. Examples of commonly used well known 100% equity index funds are:

- Vanguard US Index
- Vanguard Lifestrategy 100% Equity
- HSBC FTSE All-Share Index
- Fidelity Index World

And many, many others. The key is to look for the lowest cost exposure of all the funds you can find and make sure they are invested in 100% equity. I would also try not to get too clever by picking countries such as China or regions like emerging markets. Doing this just adds an extra layer of risk that you don't necessarily need. Stick to the main developed markets like the US, UK and Europe is my tip.

So there you have it, by following these steps above you have reviewed your pensions, consolidated them and reinvested them into low-cost funds that are suitable for long-term growth. Future you just gave current you a massive high-five and will see you in your Happy Place.

There are a few other things to think about with pensions, starting with a danger sign – lifestyling.

Lifestyling

If you see the words Lifestyling or Target Date or have a year in the fund you're invested in then please take note. This is important.

What these rather benign words mean is that the funds you're invested in will automatically "de-risk" as you approach your retirement date, without you asking them or giving them approval to do so. I use "de-risk" in quotation marks because what these schemes are actually doing is moving your funds to assets such as bonds and cash that are meant to be more stable and offer very little growth prospects, sometimes even prospects that are almost guaranteed to be below inflation. The original principle behind this automated switch of assets was to give you less volatility coming into your retirement date, as the FCA would like you to use your pot to buy a guaranteed pension income from an insurance company – called an annuity. This used to be what you had to do, but now with pensions freedoms, which started in 2015, you no longer have to do this and can have total flexibility in terms of how you draw down your pension. In my mind, Lifestyling or Target Date funds no longer serve the purpose they were designed for, yet are still widely used because the pension providers feel encouraged to do so because of the regulator's view that we all "should" be buying an annuity. It's dangerous and wrong.

How dangerous? Let me give you an example.

It is estimated there is currently around £20 billion in pensions that are either lost or forgotten.[30] For the argument let us say these pensions are eventually found by people when they are in their 70s. If these pensions were invested in a Lifestyle strategy or Target Date funds, they would have been sitting in cash or cash-type equivalents, earning virtually NO return and losing money versus inflation for the previous ten or more years. Can you see how dangerous that is? If money is not growing at average growth rate of inflation or higher, it is going backwards. And these funds are forcing unaware people into this situation. So be careful of this.

Pension contributions

If you earn over £10,000 per year you will automatically be enrolled into your employer pension. That is now law. You always have the option of un-enrolling yourself, but you would

---

30 https://www.unbiased.co.uk/news/financial-adviser/billions-lost-in-forgotten-pensions

only do this in very specific situations where you don't want the extra funds.

There is a minimum contribution that your employer must pay and also a minimum contribution they must take from your salary for you to pay. At the time of writing this is 3% of your salary for your employer and 4% for you.[31] However, many employers pay different amounts to this. A good rule is to put the maximum in that will maximise the amount your company puts in.

The great thing about your pension contributions is they get tax relief. Paying money into your pension is one of the few ways to reduce your taxes. However, remember the trade-off. With any contributions you make into your pension, you cannot touch that money again until you are at least 55. Therefore you need to be careful and conscious about how much you put in.

A couple of rules of thumb that I like to use with my clients.

1. If you earn over £100,000 then you hit a tax-zone of 60% between that level and £125,000. This is because at this point your personal allowance – the first £12,500 earning being tax-free is taken away. That means you pay the normal 40% tax + 20% extra that the personal allowance would have saved you, totalling 60%. If you can make extra pension contributions in this zone, and even better to get your net taxable earnings (total earnings minus personal pension contributions) down below £100,000, then you effectively receive 60% tax relief on those contributions.

2. Are you a director of your own limited company? Pensions are a really effective way of moving funds out of the company and into your account. Normally when you do this you pay dividend or income tax, but when the company pays money direct into your pension, it moves across gross of tax. So £100 gets paid out by

---

31 Correct in tax year 2022/23

your company and £100 gets invested into your pension. And to make it even better, that £100 paid by the company is treated as a business expense so it reduces your net profit and therefore corporation tax due by the company. A win-win.

Putting extra contributions into your pension is always a balance. On one side is the positive of the tax relief and the saving for the future. On the other side is the lack of ability to get these funds back. Each individual has different needs for this, so this decision of how much extra to put in is this time up to you I'm afraid.

CHAPTER 16

Planning for Inheritance Tax

In this chapter you will learn

- *Different strategies to think about if you have elderly relatives*
- *How you can de-risk your family's situation in the event of your own death*
- *Why writing things down helps*

This bit of the book is probably the most difficult for you to read, because it's about death – the death of those dear to you and your own death. But just because something is difficult to think about doesn't mean we should ignore it. In fact, ignoring death can be extremely expensive. In the tax year 2018–19, HMRC collected £5.4 billion in inheritance tax. HMRC believes that by 2030, which is only ten years from now and in all likelihood well within the time you expect to be still alive and hope your parents will still be with us, that figure will have increased to £10 billion.

I'm the last person to suggest that we should avoid paying the tax we are liable to pay. Tax is law. But getting tax relief through sensible decision making is also law, and I, as a regulated financial planner, have a duty to my clients to legally save them as much tax as possible. So let's start looking at things you should be doing.

Precautions in respect of elderly relatives

I'll be talking shortly about what you need to do to make sure that as much as possible of what *you* leave behind goes to your chosen beneficiaries and not to HMRC. First, though, let's talk about any elderly relatives you may have – your parents, or other relatives for whom you have a responsibility – and what *they* are likely to leave behind.

Power of attorney

Perhaps the most important planning decision you can make for your elderly relatives is to make sure they have in place a power of attorney. Losing mental capacity is horrible to deal with but unfortunately it is almost inevitable for most people. Without a power of attorney in place, it becomes almost impossible to help your relatives. If there is no attorney in place and they lose capacity, then any financial decision ends up in the court of protection with normally a six-month waiting period. Nobody wants that to happen. I explain more about these later in the chapter.

Life insurance

Many, and perhaps the majority, of elderly relatives will no longer have life insurance – but some will. If yours are among them, is the insurance written into trust? If it isn't, then when the person dies and the insurance pays out, it will go straight into the deceased's estate and become subject to inheritance tax. I submit that that is not what the insured person wanted – they did not say, "I must take out insurance so that the taxman gets extra money when I snuff it." What they intended was that the money should go to the human beings mentioned in their will, and that is easy enough to arrange – just ask the insurance company for a trust document and have the insured person sign it. It would be easy not to do this for fear of reminding the insured person that their death may not be far away. Easy, but foolish. I've seen a number of cases and, each time, when the situation was explained to the insured person, they were falling over themselves to sign a trust document.

Investment properties

I said in the last chapter that I would have something to say on this subject here. You can't do much with your elderly relative's main property while they're still living in it, but investment properties are different. If your relative doesn't rely on the income then these properties can be gifted to another family member (or multiple members). If they are reliant on the income, then you cannot do this. I explain why below.

As this is not technically a sale, then there is no stamp duty charged, but all other legal costs of selling a property should be considered. As long as the elderly relative is still alive, liability for inheritance tax on this gift will begin to reduce after four years and after seven years it will be gone. If ever there was a clear case for acting earlier rather than later, that's it!

In all inheritance tax planning, you have to be very careful around what is called a 'gift with reservation', which in layman's terms means you can't have your cake and eat it too! This means you cannot give away an asset and still receive benefit of it. If that happens then the asset will still be included in the estate for inheritance tax purposes. This simplest case that most people think about is gifting your parents' house to the children, but the parents still live in there. If this happened, then this counts as a gift-with-reservation and the house would be counted as part of the parents' estate even though they don't technically own it anymore. One way around this particular example is for the parents to pay a market rate of rent. HMRC will sometimes check on this so it's worth being careful.

ISAs

Great as they are as tax-free options for income and growth while the holder is alive, on death they form part of the estate and are therefore liable for inheritance tax. One option is to switch an elderly relative's ISA(s) into another ISA-based investment that qualifies for business property relief (or BPR). BPR's main advantage is that its assets become exempt from inheritance tax after only two years, against the normal seven for gifts. Another benefit is that the investment will always be held in the elderly relative's name (because they're not giving the funds away) and they can always access them again if required.

Pensions

The treatment on death of pensions entirely depends on why type of pension it is.

The older-style final salary pension normally dies with the person, although they may have a spouse pension or child pension attached to it. The rules for each are set out in the terms of each pension.

For the more modern defined contribution pension the rules are clearer. These pensions will very rarely form part of the estate on death. Yes, that's correct so let me repeat that in another way. It is highly unlikely you will pay inheritance tax on a pension pot. As pensions are outside of the estate, they then offer distinct inheritance tax planning opportunities. Given a choice between taking money out of the pension and taking money from cash/savings, then from an inheritance perspective it is normally better to leave the pension alone.

But wait, it also gets more interesting. If the pension pot holder dies before age 75, then the entire remaining pension fund can be paid tax-free to the beneficiaries. That's right, no tax at all. If the death occurs at 75 or older, then the fund is still outside of the estate and passed over to beneficiaries without inheritance tax, but the beneficiaries will need to pay their marginal rate of income tax when they draw the fund down. The other important tax point, is this beneficiary pension, as it will now be called, does not count towards the lifetime allowance of the beneficiary.

These new pension rules only came in around 2015 so they are all very new and relatively unknown, but can make a big difference to passing wealth down if understood properly.

Cash and shares

There are two ways to deal with this and you will need expert advice for either of them. I'm going to explain what they are and how they work so that, when you go to talk to a solicitor, you know what you're talking about – but, please, don't skip the visit to the solicitor. You don't want everything to go wrong when it's too late to do anything about it because the person who owned the cash and/or shares is dead.

The first thing you can do is to put the cash and/or shares into a trust. Fine. So what's a trust? A trust is an arrangement under which the person with the cash gives it to someone else (the trustee(s)) to manage on behalf of the person whose money it is. You could, of course, simply hand it to them with instructions about what they were to do with it, but then you run the risk that they will use it for something else, and there's also the problem that the money will be treated as a taxable gift. Your elderly relative might set up a trust in order:

So that it can be looked after properly when they are no longer able to do so;

To provide themselves an income in a tax-efficient manner;

To transfer money to their children in the most tax-efficient way without giving the children total control of it; *or*

So that the taxman doesn't get any more of the money on the person's death than they are entitled to.

There are other uses, such as providing a way for a person with a mental health problem or a learning disability to receive state benefits but have them go straight to the trustees who will administer the funds on their behalf, but those uses of a trust are not relevant to our purposes here.

You can structure a trust in many different ways and there are many different trusts you can use. Qualified advice here is important – you can either use a financial planner or a solicitor. Both will charge, and I may be biased but I would suggest using a financial planner as they can help you on the investment strategy as well. Trust and inheritance tax planning forms an important part of the training for financial planners so they should know their stuff.

A key attribute of a trust is that the funds are not looked after by the original donor (or settlor) but by trustees, who are chosen at the outset. You need to choose who the trustees are going to be. Ideally, you want a minimum of two and a maximum of four and you need to be sure that they are people you can trust. A large trust can be a source of terrible temptation. Alternatively, you can choose a bank or a firm of solicitors to be your trustee, but bear in mind that they will charge.

If the elderly relative is no longer able to care for him or herself and needs care, you may want to apply on their behalf for the council to pay some or all of their care costs. One of the things they will look at will be how much money and other assets the elderly relative has, and they will look at both the capital in the trust and the income derived from it. The extent to which these are taken into account when assessing how much the council will pay depends on how the trust is worded. That on its own should encourage most people to take expert advice.

An alternative to trusts is Business Property Relief, which was dealt with under ISAs above. A stable investment such as asset-backed loans would be a suitable vehicle but, once again, expert advice is essential.

Precautions in respect of you
Everything in this chapter so far has been about how to make sure that an elderly relative is able to pass on as much as possible of the assets they own after they die. But what about you? You're going to die too.

So what do you have to do to make sure that as much as possible of what you have when your life comes to an end is passed on to your heirs? Exactly the same as you needed to do for your elderly relatives. Just take everything from the beginning of this chapter to here and apply it to your own assets. The words to have in mind are:

Being prepared
Logic says that this should come at the beginning of this chapter – but my experience says that what people want to know most of all is what they need to do in practice to keep inheritance

tax to a minimum. Now that we've done that, it's time to make sure that you're ready when the time comes. The time for your elderly relatives – and the time for you.

A client told me that he had received a call from his mother some years ago. She said, 'I thought you ought to know, I've paid for my funeral.'

'Oh,' said my client. 'Have you fixed the date?'

An amusing response off the cuff, and as it turned out the client's mother lived another 33 years because she was 70 when she paid the Co-op Funeral Services for her funeral and 103 when she finally made use of it, so she certainly got value for money. But I'm with the mother; at 70 she didn't know how much longer she had, but she'd seen the departure of enough people her own age to know that she wasn't going to live forever. So – she prepared.

Being prepared is not only for Boy Scouts. When there's going to be a wedding in the family, we make all the preparations, decide who's going to be the best man and who will be bridesmaids, we book the church and the venue, draw up a gift list and send out invitations. When a birth is expected, we paint the baby's bedroom, buy nappies and baby clothes, get a pram and a pushchair and attend regular antenatal check-ups. And yet, so often, we fail to prepare for death (our own or that of someone close to us), even though death is unavoidable while marriage is optional and having children may never happen.

Here is what you need to do, for elderly relatives and for yourself. Go through the filing cabinets and/or the PC and find the following documents:

- Will
- Powers of attorney
- Investments and share certificates
- Digital assets
- Bank accounts
- Insurance policies
- Property deeds

- Solicitors/Accountants/IFA details
- Pensions
- Bills

All of these documents should be reviewed and kept in a secure file and tell the people who need to know where it is. It may be helpful to create a 'Financial Passport' with all this information in one easy to use document. You can download a copy from our website at (www.adamwalkom.com). Going through probate is never fun for anyone but if you can reduce the administration side down to the minimum stress possible, it should make it easier. To complete the passport, you need to know where all of these things are for anyone whose estate you are likely to be asked to administer, and you need to know where your own are (and you need to make sure that someone else knows, too). Let's go through them.

Will

Have you made a will? If not, why not? I'm sorry, but this is inexcusable. The number of times I hear "Well it will just all go to my partner, won't it?" always finishing that sentence with a small amount of uncertainty. Yes, on your death, it may all go to your partner, but do you really want them to deal with the hassle of collating everything and working out how much to report to HMRC? In the emotional state they are most likely to be at that point? No, I didn't think so. A key part of the will is nominating an executor who has the responsibility to do that and leaving your partner to grieve. Surely that is the considerate thing to do.

And have elderly relatives for whom you will be responsible made wills? If not, make your own and ensure that the relatives make theirs. This is not optional. There is no other way to make sure that all the assets are disposed of and all the bills paid exactly as you or your relative would wish unless there is a will that says what those wishes are. Make sure you know where your relative's will is, and that your executor knows where yours is. Don't put it off.

Powers of attorney

A power of attorney gives one person the right to act on behalf of another. Powers of attorney may be General or Lasting and the one we are concerned with here is a Lasting Power of Attorney. A Lasting Power of Attorney gives another person the right to make decisions on your behalf when you are unable to do so either because of illness, accident or mental incapacity. It's best to make one before you need it because, if mental incapacity is already affecting you, you won't be able to make one. You can download forms from the web (just Google 'Lasting Power of Attorney') and you have to register it with the Office of the Public Guardian and pay a fee which at the time of writing is £82. The most important powers that can be given under a Lasting Power of Attorney are to:

- Manage a bank or building society account
- Pay bills
- Collect benefits or a pension
- Sell your home

Sometimes I see a reluctance to take on the power of attorney role as some people think they may be at risk if they make the wrong decision. From a legal standpoint you are obliged to make the best decision for your relative, so in a lot of ways this protects you. There can be no misinterpreting any decision, as it always has to be in their best interest.

There are powers of attorney for both health decisions and financial decisions but I won't go into any more detail here other than to say they are very important. Please speak to a solicitor about these.

Bank accounts

It's no good having a Lasting Power of Attorney that authorises you to manage someone else's bank or building society accounts if you don't know where the accounts are. Apart from which, one of the very first things you need to do when someone dies is to inform their bank. You won't be able to do that without the bank details. Okay, it's likely that bank statements will arrive after the account holder's death, but waiting for that to happen is not being prepared. Find out now. And, for your own accounts, make sure that your executor knows.

Investments and share certificates, property deeds and insurance policies

Imagine the frustration of knowing the relative for whom you are acting has shares, ISAs, a GIA or other forms of investment – and you can't do anything with them, because you don't know where they are. Imagine your own executor's frustration at being in the same position in relation to your investments and not being able to ask you because you have been taken away in a closed wooden box. Find out where your relative's shares are before he or she passes on. Make sure your executor knows where to find yours. The same goes for the deeds to property and for insurance policies.

Digital

For one moment just consider how much of a digital footprint you will leave behind if you were not here anymore.

As our lives become ever more digital, so are the records that are kept online in terms of everything we do.

Importantly on your death, digital assets do NOT automatically become part of your estate and therefore distributed to your beneficiaries. If you do not specify this, they will become the property of Apple, Google or whoever holds these.

The key digital assets to consider are:

- Photos on your mobile phone or PC
- Emails
- Social Media accounts
- Digital money, either Paypal or crypto accounts
- Music or Games
- Business assets

None of this was an issue 20 years ago, but has become much more important today. Having an inventory of these assets, along with how they be accessed should be stored alongside your will.

Pensions

When someone dies while in receipt of a pension (both state and private), the executor should inform the payer of the pension without delay. That means the name of the payer, the name of the beneficiary and any reference numbers need to be immediately available.

Solicitors/Accountants/IFA details

If the deceased person (whether it's a relative or you) has an accountant, a solicitor or an independent financial adviser, it's almost certain that that person will be able to answer any questions concerning any of the above. So, if there is such a person, make sure his or her name, work address, email address and phone number are readily available.

CHAPTER 17

Is Debt a Bad Thing?

In this chapter you will learn

- *The pros and cons of debt – especially a mortgage*
- *The longer-term history of U.K. interest rates and where we sit now*
- *Strategies to deal with paying down mortgage in a higher interest rate environment*

The phrase "Is debt a bad thing?" generally stirs an interesting reaction. Some, naturally, are inclined to shriek "Yes!" as the merest hint of debt causes their stomachs to seize up with nervous fear along with a mental image of heavy cast iron shackles pinning them down. And with the events of 2008 so recent in everyone's subconscious, this is fully understandable.

However, as a financial planner, I get to see all sorts of clients in all sorts of situations and sometimes debt, if managed properly, can be a very positive financial planning tool and can, if sensibly used, improve people's lives.

One example that comes to mind is the dreaded student loan. The newspapers tend to be filled with students (or interestingly parents) complaining about how they are "burdened" and "saddled" and other visually loaded phrases with significant debts on graduation from university. However, if you want to go to university to improve your career prospects and your parents cannot or will not pay for you, then a student loan can be a very sensible debt to take on. The benefits of a loan are that it should improve your earning potential in the future, the payments are restricted until you are earning a certain amount, plus the balance is potentially written off if you have not fully repaid it in 25 years. With the potential to significantly improve your standing in life, that sounds like a pretty good deal to me.

A mortgage is another debt which we all know gives you a chance to not only get on the housing ladder, but increase the quality of your property in the future. Rates go up and down but the mortgage market is very competitive so often you can find some very good deals. It pays to shop around and even potentially look at using a mortgage broker. Yes, the charge but they often get access to better deals from smaller building societies that you or I will never find.

The flip side of this debt discussion though is credit card debt. Useful for liquidity, yes – however the downsides and risks of credit card debt are well documented and rightly so. When you're paying 29.9% interest, it's no wonder people can get themselves in a horrible cycle of only just being able to afford the interest. This is to be avoided at all costs.

The issue of debt is a very personal subject and clearly advice will be different for people depending on their circumstances and stage of life. If you want to understand what options are available to you, speaking with a financial adviser can provide you with professional guidance when it comes to managing it.

Should I overpay my mortgage?

Interest rates are rising. We all know that. If we aren't already, all of us are going to be paying far more on mortgage repayments than we have for a very long time.

As this is one of the most common questions we get asked and the answer is not as simple as perhaps it should be, I felt it was worth unpacking here in a more long-form way.

Let's start by looking at interest rates since the mid-1970s.

Bank of England base rates since 1975

I'm using this timeframe because the 1970s and 80s were the last time that we had inflation as high as it currently is. So, there is an argument that interest rates are still very low.

But remember that people don't get the Bank of England rate when taking out mortgages. We get some derivation of, either fixed for a while, or linked to the movement of the underlying rate.

This chart below shows the average standard variable rate (SVR) in the U.K over the last 20+ years

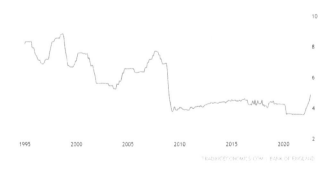

Interestingly, even during the recent 0% base rate environment, standard variable rates (SVRs) didn't get much below 4%. However, the majority of mortgage holders have deals at

lower fixed or variable rates and don't have to pay these higher SVRs. The problem is though that these deals are rolling off now and will continue to do so over the next few years. At this point, a large number of mortgage holders will find themselves re-mortgaging at much higher rates.

Whilst paying higher interest rates is not much fun, should this change your overall economic plan? It depends on your priorities.

For some people, their principal financial goal is to own their own house, and they focus almost religiously on paying down the mortgage. That's fine and a reasonable strategy if it gives you the most comfort. Others view their mortgage as more part of their overall plan and are happy to have the debt as it allows them a larger house and they feel they can make higher returns on the funds elsewhere. Both are personal choices so have specific utility value for the individual making the decision.

Here are a few examples and scenarios of ways you can think about it. These scenarios are not based on any specific clients, but are more generalist in nature to give you an idea on a few ways to think about mortgage repayments.

Scenario 1 – Large mortgage, mortgage deal expiring in a few years.

This scenario sees a client who has relatively recently upsized their family home and taken on a large mortgage to go along with it. They are still on a relatively attractive deal at the moment, though that will end in 2–3 years. These clients have other assets, investments, pensions etc. and are on track for their financial goals.

Potential strategy – De-risking.

As this client is on track and sees no reason why income should fall anytime soon, a way to think about mortgage repayments would be to look across their financial situation and ask "What is the biggest risk we face and how can we reduce this?" A high mortgage level, even though its currently on a good deal, presents itself as the biggest risk to their situation. So, we can look to either start putting cash aside today, or given that markets have already had a good sell-off over the last few months, set aside an investment amount that then can be used to move over to the mortgage when they roll off their deal. The closer we get to the deal ending, the more conservative they should be with their cash and/or investments so we can make sure we can the cash in place to pay down a chunk of that mortgage as the deal expires.

Scenario 2 – Deal expiring shortly.

This scenario is where clients have a mortgage which is just coming into its deal expiry. There are no other changes to their situation, and while the client has cash and other investments and is relatively on-track, they still need to put funds away for the future.

Potential strategy – Pay down mortgage with available cash.

The rates available today start at around 3.5% and then will soon go higher as the Bank of England continues to forecast interest rate rises. If we consider this 3.5% as a "guaranteed" tax-free return on the investment in the mortgage, then that starts to become very interesting. Markets are very volatile at present and whilst they may come roaring back at some point, this still makes a fixed return more attractive. The argument could be you are still locking in a low rate whilst inflation is well above this level, but asset prices are not following inflation at this point and this inflation level will come down over the next 12 months or so. Switching cash ISAs or premium bonds over to the mortgage could even be considered at this point, but we would just need to be aware of the liquidity issues that may raise.

Scenario 3 – Relatively small mortgage, no plans on moving.

This scenario is normally for slightly older clients, where they have paid down their mortgage over the years and are left with say less than 25% of the loan-to-value outstanding.

Potential strategy – Let it ride as long as the mortgage is on a repayment plan.

If the change in mortgage payments doesn't inhibit lifestyle or further savings plans and you're still investing for the future, then perhaps it is better just to leave the mortgage as it is. As long as the mortgage is on a repayment plan it really just will take care of itself, which allows you to continue to utilise surplus cash to continue to build your wealth for retirement at some point in the future.

Obviously each scenario above is entirely theoretical and the right advice will always depend on your personal circumstances, however hopefully this has given you some frameworks to consider.

CHAPTER 18

Investment Ideas for Children

In this chapter you will learn

- *My preferred options for investing for children*
- *The type of investment strategy most suitable for children*
- *Why the financial education may be more valuable to the child than the money itself*

Any parent likes to think that the more you invest into your children, the better outcomes you can expect. This works for time, patience, love and many other factors. But it also works for another factor that is slightly less obvious – finance.

Investing FOR your children offers the chance to give your child a big financial boost when inevitably they become adults. University fees, first cars, gap years, even a deposit for a first house may feel like a lifetime away for your children, but starting saving and investing earlier gives you a big head start towards any and all of those milestones.

What are the best options to consider when investing for your child?

Junior ISAs
As simple and effective as normal ISAs, Junior ISAs are the number one investing tool for your children. The limit (as at 22/23 tax year) is £9,000 per child per year, which can go a long way.

ISAs are tax-free forever, which means all dividends, income and capital gains are not taxed.

Junior ISAs have a couple of unique characteristics you need to be aware of though:

- Once the money goes into a Junior ISA, you cannot get it out until the child turns 18. So the idea of people raiding children's Junior ISAs to fund house moves unfortunately doesn't work.
- The Junior ISAs will legally become a normal ISA on the child's 18th birthday, which means they can do with it what they like.

I have heard many comments that parents don't want their children getting access to all that money at age 18, for fear of them buying a Porsche and wrapping it around a tree. However, I have a different view. I think one of the best investments we can make for our children is educating them about finance.

I speak from personal experience.

My grandmother bought me some shares when I was about 14 years old. I still remember them – Macmahon Holdings – a small Australian engineering company and, for me, it started the journey of a lifetime. Every day I would look in the paper and track the ups and downs of those shares over time. To be honest, I think I have tracked share prices virtually every day of my life since then.

Starting that process though, taught me many things about investing and markets. It taught me that shares go up and down and how I need to embrace volatility for long-run gains. It taught me what dividends were and the benefits of compounding over time. It taught me that single company risk can be diversified away through a portfolio of investments, with the ultimate diversified portfolio being an index fund.

All of this I learned by experience and doing, both of which are much, much more effective learning tools that simply trying to read a book, or worse, my parents trying to tell me!

And it's not just me. I have had the exact same conversation with many clients. Those that have been exposed to investments and shares and the ups and downs of markets over the years, tend to make better, more relaxed and therefore more profitable investors.

Junior SIPPs

The next best option is a Junior Self-Invested Personal Pension (SIPP). A Junior SIPP is a very early pension for your child. Normal pension rules apply, in that the child, then adult, cannot access these funds before they turn 55. Once the child turns 18, like the ISA above, the Junior SIPP turns into a normal adult SIPP with all the same rules applying.

The unique aspect about Junior SIPPs are anyone can make contributions and each contribution will receive 20% tax relief. The maximum amount that can be invested each year into a Junior SIPP is £2,880 – which then becomes £3,600 with the 20% tax relief applied.

The other very attractive factor to consider with Junior SIPPs is the benefit of what Albert Einstein called the eighth wonder of the world – compounding.

As an example, if you contributed the maximum £2,880 per year to a child's Junior SIPP for the first 18 years of their life, then simply left the money alone in an investment earning 5% per year, by the time the child turns 65, that pension pot is worth over £1m. If the pot grows at 7%, which is more typical, but still below the long-term average of major stock indices like the FTSE 100 or the S&P 500, then the pot is worth over £3m!

Premium Bonds

The final option is not exactly an investment, it's more of a savings account. And to be honest, I'm not much of a fan.

Premium Bonds have been part of the UK personal finance landscape for decades and they tend to retain their popularity through the idea that people may "win" the £1m bonus that they apparently pay out. I'm sure they do, but I've never heard of anyone actually winning it. The most I've ever heard anyone get from Premium Bonds is a prize of £500. And that was just one person once.

For those that don't know, Premium Bonds are a savings-type account that doesn't pay interest, but runs random prize draws every month and pays out "prizes" ranging from £25 up to £1 m. There are plenty of £25 prizes offered but only 1x £1 m draw. The overall average savings rate changes over time and is at the time of writing 2.2% – however remember this is where the law of averages starts to hurt. Yes, the average may be 2.2% but that includes the 1 x £1 m prize draw which obviously only one person wins. If you take that out, and most people clearly will not win the £1 m, then the average savings rate is lower.

Also consider the compounding as well. Unless you choose to reinvest the prizes, you don't get any compounding benefit either. The one benefit around Premium Bonds are the prizes paid out are tax-free.

CHAPTER 19

Insurance – the Most Important Investment

In this chapter you will learn

- *Why insurance is so important*
- *The different types of insurance options available and what they cover*

When the subject of protection or insurance (also known as life assurance or critical illness cover as examples) most people tend to avoid thinking about it because, frankly, it's quite scary.

What will happen to my family if I was to die? Would they have enough? What would happen to the mortgage? All of these are very difficult questions that our brains are designed to avoid thinking about. As we are all too acutely aware, everything, and I mean everything, can change in the blink of an eye. This chapter is not about foretelling horrible events. It is about making sure the thinking and planning is done beforehand to leave you ready for anything that life may throw at you.

In my role, I'm very lucky as I talk to clients a lot about the good things they want to do. How they're growing their pensions, what are the best investments to make to build their assets, etc. However, in terms of planning it is just (some would say more) important to put the plans in place in case things weren't going to go so well. There's no point putting away £100 per month into an ISA, if you're going to need that money at some point soon to live off because you've had to stop work because of an accident.

A way to think about insurance is that it is like oxygen. You don't realise how important it is until you really need it. The problem most people have with insurance is that the market is so varied, with lots of confusing options and it can be hard to determine which policy is appropriate for you. That's where I can help. Different insurance contracts are suitable for different situations and below I will try to breakdown the different types available and what they each look to achieve.

When thinking about family protection, these are a few points you should consider:

1 – Do we have enough to cover the mortgage?
This should be the starting point for every conversation. If you have a joint mortgage and one of you dies, the mortgage will be retested against the income of the survivor. If that doesn't pass their test, the bank could foreclose and kick the surviving spouse and children out of the family home. This is an absolute must have in terms of minimum cover for a family.

2 – How will we cover living expenses with one income?
The next stage of conversation. If you were to either become seriously ill or die, how will the family live on one income? Will you need more to cover childcare expenses because the surviving spouse is working?

3 – Can I guarantee my pension and long-term investment plan?
Unfortunately you can't guarantee performance, but you can guarantee against loss or disruption of the plan because of death and/or illness. If an investment or savings plan is in place why not think about spending a few more Pounds to cover it against the worst case scenario?

4 – What if my employer gives me the insurance as a benefit package?

The problem with death-in-service benefits is they are normally paid out as a pension and therefore tested against your lifetime allowance. If you're either a high earner or have a reasonable value pension, the value you have receive from this benefit may be cut significantly because of the lifetime allowance test. Personal cover does not get paid out this way.

5 – Can I cover my grandchildren?

Absolutely. Even if you don't need the cover, perhaps the greatest gift grandparents can give is ensuring their children and grandchildren have adequate cover in place. The person paying the premium doesn't have to be the one who receives the benefits.

People are very happy to make sure their car is insured, their home, their pet and even their mobile phone. So why don't people think more about making sure their family is properly insured?

When thinking about insurance there are many different confusing options to consider

Let me run through the main types of insurance.

Insuring against Death

Life

Life insurance (or assurance as it is known in the UK) is the most basic form of insurance, where your estate will receive a lump sum pay out on your death. This is also sometimes called Whole of Life cover. Premiums can be fixed (or guaranteed) for the whole policy, or can be set for either five or ten years, then increased after then to reflect the new age of the insured.

Suitable for: Protecting your family from an early death, planning for any Inheritance Tax.

Term

Term assurance is virtually the same as life cover, except the contract is limited to a predetermined number of years rather than the whole life. If you do not die within the term of the contract, there will be no pay out and normally you will not receive your premiums back.

Suitable for: Where a lump sum investment requires protecting for a number of years.

Decreasing term assurance

A term assurance contract as above except the sum assured decreases over the term i.e., it may start off at £200,000 but then decrease by £20,000 per year over ten years. This contract has many different uses such as:

- Family Income Benefit: An insurance contract that pays the surviving family a guaranteed income for the rest of the term of the policy.
  Suitable for: Popular with families who want to protect themselves whilst the children are still at a dependent age (normally up to 21)
- Mortgage Protection: A contract that covers both the remaining interest and principal payments of an outstanding mortgage (typically over 25 years)
  Suitable for: Popular with families who want to ensure that whatever happens, they will not be forced out of the family home.
- Gift inter vivos: A contract that covers the potential tax liability from a gift or transfer out of an estate.
  Suitable for: Older people who are looking to reduce the impact of inheritance tax on their estate.

Insuring against sickness

Critical illness cover

A lump sum pay out on diagnosis of a prespecified illness from a list contained in the terms of the policy. Normally the list is very comprehensive but each policy may be slightly different. This contract is often combined with life assurance to make it relatively cheaper.

Suitable for: People concerned about the significant cost of getting sick and being off work from a major illness

Income protection insurance

Or sometimes called Permanent Health Insurance (PHI), this policy runs up until retirement age and will pay out a weekly or monthly income if you become unable to work. It normally pays between 50–60% of your current earnings for the period you are judged to be unable to work. An advantage with this policy is that you can claim multiple times up to retirement age without any change in the underlying terms.

Suitable for: People worried about how they will fund their lifestyle if they are unable to work. This can be particularly important for self-employed people, or others without other employer-provided sickness benefits.

Short-term income protection

Formerly known as Accident, Sickness and Unemployment insurance (ASU) it has two key differences to Income Protection above. First it is limited to a maximum of two years once the claim is submitted and secondly it covers involuntary unemployment as well. This policy is normally cheaper than regular Income Protection because it has a maximum term of two years.

Suitable for: Workers nervous about being made redundant or getting sick and are just looking for a policy that offers them a stop-gap. Warning – these policies have become much more expensive in the last few years as many providers have stopped coverage.

Long-term care insurance

This policy is designed to cover the spiralling costs of care homes. Average annual care home fees in London are £38,500 in 2022 and are only expected to rise. The NHS covers nursing care, but unless you have assets under £23,250 (as at 2022), then you need to pay for everything else yourself.

Suitable for: Older people who are looking to remove the worry about paying for the nursing home in the future.

Insuring against inheritance tax

Whole of life insurance

Just like normal life insurance, whole-of-life cover pays out an agreed lump sum on the death of the insured. The difference is that this policy doesn't have an end date and is guaranteed to pay out. The policy is normally linked to rise with inflation or some other measure as the aim is to pay out a sum of money to help pay for the inheritance tax bill left behind. As the policy is guaranteed to pay out, it can get very expensive by the later years as the insurance company will want to cover their costs before the pay out.

Suitable for: Families looking at planning options to help fund a potentially large inheritance tax bill.

Insuring for business

There are many varied types of business insurance that can cover all sorts of risks in running a business. From death of the directors to insurance covering key staff to shareholder protection to help the surviving spouse realise value from the business on the death of the founder or major shareholder, there are too many different forms to cover here in one chapter. If this is relevant to you, my suggestion would be to Google your question or speak to a financial adviser. There can be distinct tax advantages from putting the insurance cover through the company.

Suitable for: Limited company directors and major shareholders of small-to-medium-size businesses.

The above are just some of the insurance options available and most contracts are flexible in terms of adjusting premiums or increasing the amount insured with either inflation or another index.

Remember insurance is the one investment you never want to pay off, but my goodness, it could be the most important investment you've ever made.

CHAPTER 20

Avoiding the Most Common Mistakes

In this chapter you will learn

- *Common mistakes most investors make with their finances*
- *And, most importantly, how to avoid them.*

One of the hardest to quantify, yet single most important roles I have as a financial planner is to help stop clients making mistakes.

Now these could be the everyday type mistakes of forgetting to put into your ISA or accidently overpaying into your pension. Or they could be the life-changing catastrophic mistake that changes everything.

Use this book as your guard. If you've got questions on something, or considering making a financial decision, check what it says in the book. It may be able to help, or it may not, however hopefully it may just avoid you doing something which has significant consequences.

You can do everything right, year in, year out, then on a whim decide that an advertisement that says "guaranteed 12% return" seems genuine (note: It's not). You hear of the number of very sensible people who get scammed and they shouldn't be ashamed. The scammers use sophisticated psychological tricks to get people to act in a certain way. However, if I can help stop that, then I've hopefully just saved you something like 1000x the cost that of this book.

The other common mistakes tend to be more behavioural. Investing is not natural to our biology. We exist as a species because of risk aversion and moving with the crowds, ironically two of the worst things you can do as an investor. See if any of the following sound similar…

"There's too much political risk, I'd like to wait it out a bit".

There is always political risk. But Putin, but Trump, but Brexit, but the election…. Markets ignore politics.

"The markets are falling, I'm going to wait until they stabilise"

So instead of buying at £10 you would prefer to buy at £15. Sounds crazy when you say it that way, but that is what natural human instinct tells us to do.

"I don't need a long-term plan, my money will look after itself".

Days are long but decades go by very quickly. Remember when you turned 18 and thought you were all grown up? Exactly my point.

"I can beat the market with my own stock/fund picks"

It is a miracle if a part-time investor can beat highly incentivised professional investors who have been doing this full-time their whole career. Or just luck. And luck doesn't last.

"I'll just pay the minimum balance this month and then start paying it off next month"

Tomorrow is too late. Always start what you can today.

As a financial planner I wear many hats. The hat which stops clients making errors is absolutely the most important one. It doesn't get worn often, but when it does, it is easily the most valuable part of what we do.

CHAPTER 21

The Simple Rules of Finance

To finish up I want to bring this all together. We've gone into lots of details through the book and you are now ready to go out and find that Happy Place. Remember we need to Plan for Happy. It may be helpful to boil this down to the simplest possible explanation. What are the simple rules we can use to make our lives easier?

Life is so busy and complex in so many areas, if we can just anchor ourselves around a few simple ideas for the basic areas such as personal finance, this allows our brains to concentrate on all the other things.

The other advantage of simple rules is they tend to be also home truths, as in tried-and-tested rules. These are the type of rules that your Grandmother probably told you when you were small, which were told to her by her Grandmother etc. which is why they tend to be correct.

Nothing complex here, but just straight-forward ideas that I'm sure you've heard before, we just forget or choose to ignore them. These rules are quite personal to me, but if you have any others you like to live by, please feel free to share. Here goes:

- Don't spend more than you earn.
- Keep a safety net of cash for emergencies.
- Tax relief matters. Maximise ISAs, minimise Income tax and CGT where possible.

- The markets are for long-term growth. If you need the funds within the next few years, better to be in cash savings.
- Debt is not always a bad thing, but needs to be monitored very carefully.
- Markets climb a wall of worry – if everyone around you is bearish then it's probably a good sign.

And most importantly..

- Be a good person. It just helps everything.

There is no rocket science in any of the above points, just simple rules that I find handy to remember whenever a decision needs to be made. Try it and feel free to let me know the rules you live by to make life easier.

CHAPTER 22

What are you Waiting for?

Remember this chart?

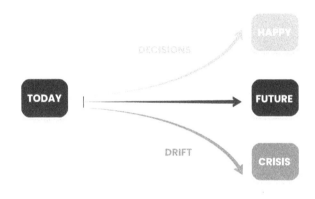

Back in Chapter 3 we discussed the difference between your Happy Place and Crisis was the difference between letting things drift and taking active decisions.

You've taken the first active decision by reading this book to the end. Congratulations. Your future self and your family will be forever grateful for that.

Now, if you haven't already, your job is to take this further. To really firmly fix that picture of your Happy Place in your mind and start putting the work in to get there.

It won't be easy, but I've given you the playbook here to get you through.

I wish you all the best on your journey and let me know how you go through getting in touch through the website www. adamwalkom.com

SUPPLEMENTARY SECTION

Different Investment Structures Available

Individual Savings Accounts (ISAs) – a tax-free account where you can put a maximum of £20,000 in per person per tax year. Once the money is in the account, all returns – be they interest income, dividends or capital gains are tax-free and need to be declared on the tax return. The main type of ISAs are Investment ISAs which are also sometimes called Stocks & Shares ISAs.

Cash ISAs – same rules, but they only hold cash. These are basically pointless as why waste valuable tax-free growth on cash which doesn't grow? The only benefit of Cash ISAs is that they can be transferred into Investment ISAs over and above the annual £20,000 allowance.

Lifetime ISA (used to be called Help to Buy ISAs) – only available if you're aged between 18 and 40. The maximum investment is £4,000 per year and the Government will add another 25% (max £1,000). This investment does count towards your overall £20,000 ISA allowance. You can withdraw your funds with no penalty when you 1) buy your first house or 2) are aged 60 and over or 3) are terminally ill with less than 12 months to live. If you withdraw the funds for any other reason the Government will charge you 25% of the fund to do so.

Innovative Finance ISA – this is an ISA used for peer-to-peer lending. From a personal point of view, I really don't like peer-to-peer lending because of the risk/return payoff. You are lending to high-risk start-up style businesses (call it an equity-style risk), but only get a fixed pay out if they stay in business (call this a fixed interest return). You get no additional benefit if the company does well; you just get your money back and an interest payment. But, if the company goes bankrupt, which as a higher-risk small company is by no means unlikely, then you lose all your money. It just doesn't make sense to me.

General Investment Account (GIA) – These are relatively straightforward taxable investment accounts. You can invest an unlimited amount into them, but you are subject to tax on this account. You do, though, receive all your tax reliefs such as dividend tax allowance (£1,000 in 2023–24), interest allowance (either £500 or £1,000 in 2023–24) and capital gains tax allowance (£6,000 in 2023-24).

Your GIA and ISA should be linked on the same platform to make it easier to:

1. have the same investments in both;
2. see everything together; *and*
3. take £20,000 from your GIA and use that to fund your ISA allowance each year – this practice is rather strangely called a Bed & ISA.

Even though there is no maximum to your GIA, we do need to be a little strategic in terms of the amount we invest. This is because we don't want to cause any unintended tax issues and costs by going over the different tax reliefs offered. To be safe and as a relatively round figure, we can assume that an amount of roughly £200,000 per person in a GIA should reduce the risk of paying tax each year. The area to watch out for is the dividends, so if the fund/share you've invested in pays more than 1% dividend (1% of £200,000 is £2,000 which is the maximum dividend allowance), then you may owe some tax. Look carefully at your investment funds to determine this. The other issue to watch is capital gains, because anything above a 3% gain on this amount could push you into taxable territory if you wanted to cash out at any point. A good financial adviser will help you manage this tax position by switching between investments, but that is getting a little too detailed to describe here.

The other benefit of a GIA is you can put it in joint name. That means you can have a joint GIA with your partner and you can use both your tax reliefs which means you can effectively double the amount you can have in a GIA (in this case roughly £400,000) before tax becomes an issue.

Investment Bonds – a legacy from another time and are in fact normally single-premium life insurance policies, but can be very useful when it comes to managing tax on investments.

There are two types of investment bonds – onshore and offshore.

The key point about both of these bonds is that they are simply investment structures. The underlying funds that you invest in remain the standard UK-regulated funds that you have access to in your ISA, GIA and pensions. From that point of view, you get all the consumer protection provided by the UK regulators which is very positive. The structure of investments bonds is, though, slightly different and needs explaining.

Both types of bonds have the following attributes:

You can withdraw each year up to 5% of the amount originally invested without any tax implications as a repayment of capital. This 5% is cumulative, so if you don't withdraw anything in the first year, you can withdraw up to 10% in the 2nd year and so on. If you withdraw more than this cumulative 5%, then the gains may be taxable.

The bonds are broken into segments (normally 1,000) which can be gifted. When these segments are gifted, the bond is still intact, so if the receiver was to cash out the bonds, any tax implication would fall on them. This can be particularly useful if you are gifting the bonds from a higher to a basic (or no) rate taxpayer. An example would be a higher rate taxpayer gifting the bonds to their children to pay for their university fees.

The bonds are also seen as non-income-producing assets, so any dividends or interest they pay means you are not liable for those each tax year. When you sell you potentially become liable on the gains in ways that differ between onshore and offshore.

Onshore investment bonds are based in the UK and invest in funds which pay both income and capital gains tax. HMRC sees this as equivalent to the investor's basic rate of tax, so as long basic rate taxpayers will pay no more tax – it is seen to have been paid already by the fund. In reality it means that the fund performance is lower because tax is taken out, but you as the investor don't need to worry about declaring this tax on your tax return. If, when you sell the bond, you are a higher rate taxpayer, then you will be liable for the difference between your 40% tax rate and the 20% basic tax rate already assumed to have been paid.

Offshore investment bonds have been around since the late 1960s when the UK first set up a regulated offshore investment structure. To be clear, this is not Panama or anything dodgy. These bonds have been tested many times by HMRC who seem very comfortable with them. The bonds are normally domiciled in either the Isle of Man or Ireland which is what makes them technically offshore.

The main difference between onshore and offshore bonds is that no tax has been paid on any of the offshore funds and the tax is all on the holder when they sell the bond. This has the benefit of "gross roll-up" which is a funny way of describing the compounding effect of having no tax taken out along the way. The 5% rule still applies but the final tax is calculated by a method called top-slicing. I'm not going to even try to explain that because, if you are getting to the level where this is relevant, you really should be talking to an adviser.

The key point around this is that tax matters. You may get the underlying investment part right and invest in funds/shares that move higher, but if you have to give away a big part of those gains in tax because you got the structuring wrong, then that's just a shame.

We all have to pay tax, but we shouldn't need to overpay because we've made mistakes.

Bibliography

Bancroft.berkeley.edu. 2020. *Slaying The Dragon Of Debt – Regional Oral History Office – University Of California, Berkeley.* [online] Available at: <https://bancroft.berkeley.edu/ROHO/projects/debt/index.html> [Accessed 30 October 2020].

Boyce, C., Brown, G. and Moore, S., 2010. Money and Happiness. *Psychological Science*, 21(4), pp. 471–475.

GOV.UK. 2020. *Make, Register Or End A Lasting Power Of Attorney.* [online] Available at: <https://www.gov.uk/power-of-attorney> [Accessed 12 December 2020].

Holiday, Ryan, 2022. *Discipline is Destiny*. Profile Books

Jebb, A., Tay, L., Diener, E. and Oishi, S., 2018. Happiness, income satiation and turning points around the world. *Nature Human Behaviour*, 2(1), pp. 33–38.

Maboussin, Michael, Credit Suisse First Boston Equity Research, Get Real – Using Real Options in Security Analysis, June 23rd 1999.

MSN. 2020. *Warren Buffett Warns Against Carrying a Credit Card Balance*. [online] Available at: <https://www.msn.com/en-us/money/credit/warren-buffett-warns-against-carrying-a-credit-card-balance/ar-BB142cWC> [Accessed 29 October 2020].

Ons.gov.uk. 2020. *Estimates of The Very Old, Including Centenarians, UK – Office For National Statistics*. [online] Available at: <https://www.ons.gov.uk/peoplepopulationandcommunity/birthsdeathsandmarriages/ageing/bulletins/estimatesoftheveryoldincludingcentenarians/2002to2019> [Accessed 10 December 2020].

The Motley Fool UK. 2020. *Index Trackers Vs Managed Funds – The Motley Fool UK*. [online] Available at: <https://www.fool.co.uk/investing-basics/isas-and-investment-funds/index-trackers-vs-managed-funds/> [Accessed 30 October 2020].

The UK Stock Market Almanac. 2020. *100 Years of the FTSE All-Share Index Since 1917*. [online] Available at: <https://stockmarketalmanac.co.uk/2016/12/100-years-of-the-ftse-all-share-index-since-1917/> [Accessed 24 November 2020].

Jorgenson, Eric, The Almanac of Naval Ravikant

Holiday, Ryan, Discipline is Destiny

Taleb, Nassim Nicholas. The Bed of Procrustes

https://www.mind.org.uk/information-support/tips-for-everyday-living/money-and-mental-health/the-link-between-money-and-mental-health/#money-can-affect-mental-health

http://content.time.com/time/magazine/article/0,9171,2019628,00.html

https://www.pnas.org/doi/10.1073/pnas.2016976118

Dolores Moreno-Herrero, Manuel Salas-Velasco, José Sánchez-Campillo,Factors that influence the level of financial literacy among young people: The role of parental engagement and students' experiences with money matters, Children and Youth Services Review, Volume 95, 2018, Pages 334–351, https://doi.org/10.1016/j.childyouth.2018.10.042.

https://www.forbes.com/sites/prudygourguechon/2019/02/25/the-psychology-of-money-what-you-need-to-know-to-have-a-relatively-fearless-financial-life/

https://www.psychologytoday.com/us/blog/the-cube/202201/happiness-is-it-all-relative [accessed 26th February 2023]

https://www.inc.com/geoffrey-james/what-goal-setting-does-to-your-brain-why-its-spectacularly-effective.html

https://www.psychologytoday.com/gb/blog/dont-delay/200806/goal-progress-and-happiness

https://www.health.harvard.edu/staying-healthy/working-later-in-life-can-pay-off-in-more-than-just-income

https://www.cic.org.uk/news/older-workers-crucial-to-curbing-construction-industry-skills-gap?s=2015-12-09-older-workers-crucial-to-curbing-construction-industry-skills-gap

https://www.cnbc.com/2020/05/13/warren-buffett-cautions-against-carrying-a-credit-card-balance.html

Willink, Jocko *Discipline Equals Freedom: Field Manual*, St Martin's Press

Newmeyer, C., Warmath, D., O'Connor, G. E., & Wong, N. (2021). Is Savings Automation Helpful to Liquid Savings? It Depends on Whether You Have a Savings Habit. *Journal of Public Policy & Marketing*, 40(2), 285–297. https://doi.org/10.1177/0743915620950216

Vos, Chris *Never Split the Difference*

https://www.statista.com/statistics/970513/unworn-clothing-british-men-and-women/

https://stockmarketalmanac.co.uk/2016/12/100-years-of-the-ftse-all-share-index-since-1917/

https://www.officialdata.org/us/stocks/s-p-500/1922?amount=100&endYear=2022

Index Trackers vs Managed Funds, The Motley Fool UK, 2020

https://investor.vanguard.com/investment-products/mutual-funds/low-cost#modal-chart-desc

https://www.unbiased.co.uk/news/financial-adviser/billions-lost-in-forgotten-pensions

Milton Keynes UK
Ingram Content Group UK Ltd.
UKHW020730161223
434349UK00009B/33